Passive Income and Aggressive Retirement

Change Your Relationship With Money. Transform Your Financial Future. Attain Freedom and Independence and Retire Early

Shaun M. Durrant

© **Copyright 2020 - All rights reserved.**

The content contained within this book may not be reproduced, duplicated or transmitted without direct written permission from the author or the publisher.

Under no circumstances will any blame or legal responsibility be held against the publisher, or author, for any damages, reparation, or monetary loss due to the information contained within this book, either directly or indirectly.

Legal Notice:

This book is copyright protected. It is only for personal use. You cannot amend, distribute, sell, use, quote or paraphrase any part, or the content within this book, without the consent of the author or publisher.

Disclaimer Notice:

Please note the information contained within this document is for educational and entertainment purposes only. All effort has been executed to present accurate, up to date, reliable, complete information. No warranties of any kind are declared or implied. Readers acknowledge that the author is not engaged in the rendering of legal, financial, medical or professional advice. The content within this book has been derived from various sources. Please consult a licensed professional before attempting any techniques outlined in this book.

By reading this document, the reader agrees that under no circumstances is the author responsible for any losses, direct or indirect, that are incurred as a result of the use of the information contained within this document, including, but not limited to, errors, omissions, or inaccuracies.

Table of Contents

INTRODUCTION 1
   MINDSETS 2
      Who am I? 4

CHAPTER 1: IS PASSIVE INCOME A MYTH? 7
   TIME 8
      Time Spent Developing Sources 9
   BENEFITS OF PASSIVE INCOME 10
      More Time 11
      Reduced Uncertainty 11
      Do What You Love 12
      Independence 13
      Stability 14
   WHAT TO AVOID 15
      You Don't Need Much Money to Generate Passive Income 15
      You Need a Lot of Money 16
      It Requires no Work 17
      Passive Income Equals "Get Rich Quick" 17
      Passive Income is Easy 17
      I Have to Invest in X, Y or Z 18
      Starting a Business is Generating Passive Income 19
   THE MISTAKES THAT BEGINNERS MAKE 19
      Skipping Research 20
      Not Creating Processes 20
      Expecting Unrealistic Results 21
      Not Planning 21
      Losing Track of Expenditures 22
      Not Managing Assets 22
      Incurring Fees and Expenses 23
      Ignoring Inflation and Taxes 23
      Being Cheap 24
      Buying Something You Don't Understand 24

CHAPTER 2: THE INVESTOR'S MINDSET 27
   DETERMINATION 28
      Know Your Strengths 28
      Find Your Purpose 29

- *Practice Delayed Gratification* 30
- *Believe* 31
- *Stay Healthy* 32
- ORGANIZATION 33
  - *Plan Your Day* 34
  - *90-90-1* 35
  - *Implement the Pareto Principle* 36
- MOTIVATION 38
  - *Give Your Ideas a Chance* 39
  - *Build Anticipation* 40
  - *Start Small* 40
  - *Get Support* 40
  - *Focus on the Benefits* 41
- GOAL ORIENTED MINDSET 41
  - *Conduct a Personal Inventory* 42
  - *Time and Money* 43
  - *Research* 44

CHAPTER 3: PASSIVE INVESTING 45

- DIVIDENDS 46
  - *Indexes* 48
  - *Index Dividend Investing* 50
- ADVANTAGES OF DIVIDEND INVESTING 51
  - *Reinvestment* 51
  - *Stability* 52
  - *Diversification* 52
- INSTRUMENTS 53
  - *Index Funds* 53
  - *ETFs* 55
  - *Evaluation* 55
- BUILDING A PORTFOLIO 57
  - *Equity* 58
  - *Fixed Income* 58
  - *Real Estate* 59
  - *International Stocks* 60
  - *Allocation* 62

CHAPTER 4: ACTIVE INVESTING 65

- ADVANTAGES 68
  - *Variety* 68
  - *Opportunities* 70
  - *Freedom* 71
- INSTRUMENTS 72
  - *Stocks* 72

  Bonds 72
  Futures 73
  Options 75
  Forex 76
  ETFs 78
 KEYS TO SUCCESS 79
  Understand Your Strategy 79
  Manage Risk 80
  Use Money You Can Lose 80

CHAPTER 5: THE BEST PASSIVE INCOME MODEL 83

 MORTGAGES AND FINANCING 84
  Numbers 85
  Terms 87
  FHA 87
  Hard Money 89
 INVESTMENT STRATEGIES 90
  Wholesaling 91
  House Hacking 93
  Turnkey Rentals 95
  Flipping Properties 97
 FINANCIAL METHODS 98
  Tax Lien Investing 99
  Mortgage Notes 100
 CROWDFUNDING 103

CHAPTER 6: ROTH AND TRADITIONAL IRAS 105

 TRADITIONAL IRAS 107
 ROTH IRA 109
 SEP IRAS 113
 SIMPLE IRA 114

CHAPTER 7: MAKING MONEY USING ETFS 117

 STOCK ETFS 118
  Sector ETFs 119
  REIT ETFs 119
 BOND ETFS 120
 COMMODITY ETFS 120
 INTERNATIONAL ETFS 121
 TAXATION 121
  Dividend Taxation 123
  REIT Dividend Taxation 124
  Physical Real Estate Taxes 125

CHAPTER 8: PROFITABLE PASSIVE INCOME MODELS OUTSIDE OF REAL ESTATE AND THE MARKETS **127**

- CONTENT CREATION 127
  - *Niche Selection 130*
  - *Choosing Topics 131*
  - *Boosting Traffic 134*
  - *Nurture 135*
  - *Monetization 136*
- DROPSHIPPING AND E-COMMERCE 138
  - *Evaluating Demand 139*
  - *Sourcing and Supply 140*
  - *Crowdfund 141*
  - *Scaling Your Business 142*
- SELF-PUBLISHING 142

CONCLUSION **145**

REFERENCES **147**

IMAGE REFERENCE LIST **149**

Introduction

"Your economic security does not lie in your job; it lies in your power to produce – to think, to learn, to create, to adapt. That's true financial independence. It's not having wealth; it's having the power to produce wealth." - Stephen .R. Covey

Here's a simple question: What's your retirement plan? If you're like most people, you'll probably have planned to retire at the age of 60 or 65. You probably have a little nest egg saved up or are in the process of saving money for it. However, your entire retirement plan can probably be summed up as "Wait and hope." If this sounds pessimistic to you, then you're thinking the right way. The fact is that the average person's retirement plan is reliant on luck more than anything else. I'm saying this because their plans are entirely dependent on how external factors pan out. If the stock market manages to remain at a decent level, then they'll have economic security in their retirement. If the economy happens to crash, which it seems to do every decade or so, then up goes their savings in a puff of smoke. The seemingly lucky ones own their place of stay and thus have a roof over their heads. However, is this really an advantage? The home needs constant repairs and upkeep. It needs to be landscaped, and the pipes need to be maintained. Even if your nest egg hasn't been wiped out, you're still living on a fixed income and can hardly afford to spend frivolously. These little expenses that come out of left field add up and can make a serious dent on your budget. Some people sell their homes and earn a cash windfall. However, they soon find that the cash they earn cannot buy the lifestyle they've enjoyed over the past 30 years. They now need to move into a smaller place that doesn't have the same level of luxuries that their previous home had. Then there's the worst mistake of all.

Thanks to the advances made by medical technology and science, people are living longer than ever before. If you plan on retiring at the age of 65, there are another 30 years to go before you say goodbye to this world. If you have grandkids at the age of 65, they'll be fully grown adults with kids of their own by the time you're 95. Are you sure you're saving enough cash to last you for that long? Even if you manage to save up a million dollars and decide to live off that principle, it works out to $33,333 per year. That's around $2,800 per month. Factor in increased medical costs, and you're faced with a less than ideal scenario.

As bleak as this picture is, the reality is even bleaker. A survey conducted by Northwestern Mutual found that 15% of Americans have nothing saved for their impending retirement. Amongst people in the age groups of 39-54, 14% said they had nothing saved away and had only debt to speak of (Martin, 2019). I used the example of a million dollars, but in reality, just 17% have savings of up to $80,000 for their retirement, well short of the mark.

Mindsets

The problem here isn't that people are implementing the wrong retirement strategies or are somehow ignorant. Technically they are ignorant of a few things, but it isn't with regards to the methods of saving. The problem is with the notion of saving itself. You see, you've been lied to all your life, and you don't even know it. What was the common narrative that you were fed as you grew up? Your teachers and parents told you to study hard, find a good job, and then work until you grew old so that you could then enjoy the fruits of your labor. They didn't tell you about the economy crashing and about people losing their jobs. They didn't tell you of the turmoil that would be caused in the wake of these crises, which would result in everything becoming more expensive in the long run. They didn't tell you about America losing its preeminent position in the world, and of the increased instability this would bring. They simply couldn't. After all, their world was very different from the one we now live in. It's been a rude wake-up call to many people, and this is why so many of us are unprepared. The good news is, you've taken a great step in reading this book. The way to build wealth has changed dramatically, and in this book, I'm going to give you the best models to build a large nest egg for your retirement.

Best of all, you're going to be able to retire much before you're 65. I personally think it's absurd that someone needs to wait until they're old to "enjoy" themselves. This is a ridiculous way to live life. It's as if you're punishing yourself for all your hard work. Sure, you need to work hard, but life doesn't suddenly change when you hit the age of 60. You'll still need to find ways to occupy your time. You can't sit there in front of the television all day long. Your brain will simply rot. Instead of thinking of your life as being a stretch of work followed by a stretch of inactivity, look to integrate your finances with your desired lifestyle. What if you could play more than you work? What if you could earn enough money to travel the world and have more than enough to save for retirement? These questions sound like pipe dreams to most people, and truth be told, they are. This is because such people are not ready to dream big and to burst past the shackles they've imposed upon themselves. They're willing to remain where they are and remain uncomfortable, as undesirable as their present situation is. You are not these people. You've taken action, already and that is to be commended.

The scenarios I've described above are easily achievable. Sure, it takes hard work, but it isn't as if you need a high IQ or some secret key to unlock riches. Consistency and showing up every day are far more important than any special knowledge. You don't need to be a genius to do this, and do you need to be a graduate of an Ivy League school either. You don't need to have a network of powerful individuals at your disposal nor do you need to have special contacts with people in high places. All you need is a desire to improve your lot in life and to avoid the disastrous scenario that awaits most of the people you know.

This book will teach you how you can build income apart from your regular job. Not just any income but truly passive income. One of the traps that people fall into is to exchange their time for money. You spend a certain number of hours at your job and get paid in return. Since your time is limited, so is your income.

Passive income disconnects your time from your ability to earn money. If you don't do this, you'll keep working until the day you die. Earn money even when you sleep, and you'll amass true wealth. In this book, you're going to learn how to build passive income businesses. While the income you earn is disconnected from your time, this doesn't mean you don't need to invest time in these ventures. You'll need to build these structures and work to maintain them. Once they're up and running, you can relax a bit and move onto building another structure.

The beauty of passive income is that the first venture fuels the second one and so on in a virtuous circle. Imagine investing $1,000 into a venture and have that generate $5,000 at the end of a year. You can use this money to invest in another venture and have that generate another $2,000 per year. This is in addition to the $5,000 that is already being generated. Building passive income streams takes time, but it's time well spent. You can't expect changes overnight, but change occurs a lot sooner than you think.

Who am I?

Let me say this right off the bat: I'm not a financial advisor. What I am though, is a passive income earner. The words in this book aren't just theory. This is practical knowledge you're going to learn about. I've experimented with these models, and I've implemented them in my life, so I'm able to write this book.

My life wasn't always like this. I was one of those "work 9-5 and retire at 65" types with my head stuck in the sand. I was lucky enough to survive the multiple market crashes and economic meltdowns that have happened since the millennium dawned but they woke me up. I was also very lucky that the internet became a much more powerful force as time went on. Passive income generation through the internet is a lot easier than people think. It truly provides access to everyone irrespective of where their life is at currently. It's fully possible to earn riches overnight but I encourage you to aim to get rich slowly. This is a much more probable and safer way to get rich and build financial independence. I've spent years researching passive income models and am passionate about the subject. "Get rich quick" is not a strategy. It's an attitude that usually leads people down the wrong path. If your intention is to create riches overnight, then I'm sorry to say, this is highly unlikely to happen for you.

Instead, focus on building processes that sustain themselves, and you'll build income streams that do the same. Focus on providing value, and money will follow. Earning a million dollars per year sounds impossible. However, here's the reality of a million dollars. If you sell a $20 product to 4,166 people every month, you'll earn a million in a year. If you hike the price to $50, you need to sell it to 1,667 people every month. Sell a service or a product for $150, and you need to sell it to 555 people every month. That's 20 people per day. If these numbers sound big to you, then aim for something smaller. How would you like to earn $100,000 per year? This can be done by selling a $20 product to 14 people every day. Head over to Amazon and look at the $20 products that are being sold right now. Do you think these sell over 14 times a day? Does the sun rise from the east?

Your goals are a lot more achievable than you think. You just can't see it. So trust the process I'm about to show you and trust your ability to execute it. You already have everything you need. Let's now take that next step and dive deeper into the topic.

Chapter 1:

Is Passive Income a Myth?

The first thing for you to understand is what passive income is. Unfortunately, passive income has become a popular topic these days, and there are a lot of fake gurus trying to sell you on the idea. It's become a buzzword for a number of charlatans to sell their overpriced courses. As a result, it becomes easy to attain a warped definition of what it truly is. Passive income is income that requires little to no maintenance on your part. True passive income does require some maintenance, but the effort you expend on it isn't anywhere near the effort you exert in your active source of income.

This brings us to another term in the passive income universe. Active income is money you earn in exchange for your time. Some people have problems figuring this out, so let's use an example. If you're working at a job, you're exchanging your time for money. Sure, you think you're being paid for your qualifications and for your skills, but this isn't the case. How would your boss react if you finished a week's worth of work in a day and took the rest of the week off? They'd likely pile more work onto your plate since they cannot have a worker sitting around idly (in their mind.) You're not being rewarded with money for the quality of your work. You're being given money for spending time in the workplace. Every once in a while, you receive a promotion and raise, but it isn't as if every single action of yours contributes to this raise. Someone who spends a lot of time working for a company will be promoted over time by default. They might not rise to the level of the CEO, but they'll attain seniority nonetheless. The key thing to understand when analyzing your income is the time spent generating it.

Time

Time is precious. You have just 24 hours every day and cannot conjure additional time no matter how hard you try. From these 24 hours, you have to spend some amount of time sleeping and resting. You wouldn't be able to function otherwise. You need to spend time with your family, or else you wouldn't have much joy in your life. You need to spend time at your job, which is typically eight hours. You need to spend time eating and nourishing yourself. For the average person, this leaves around two or three hours every day that they can use to generate passive income. This might not sound like a lot but you will see rewards with consistency and regular effort. If you want to achieve financial independence, then creating passive income is absolutely necessary.

This effectively leverages your time. Leverage in financial circles is used to describe an investment that has its returns boosted in some way. A common form of leverage is debt. A person borrows money to buy something, and once the value rises, they return the money borrowed and keep all the gains for themselves. Thus they earn an outsized return on their cash invested. When it comes to time and money, leveraging the former means you're earning more dollars per hour without necessarily putting in the same effort. For example, a savings account is an example of a passive investment. It takes zero effort to earn money from it. You deposit your money, and that's it. Investing in a business as a silent partner is another example. The Internal Revenue Service (IRS) doesn't distinguish between active and passive income for tax purposes, unfortunately. It defines a passive investment as one that you have no material participation in (*Passive Income*, 2003).

For the purposes of this book, it's not important to dive into the intricacies of the internal revenue code. Just understand that money invested in a business that is being run by someone else generates passive income. However, it takes more work than a savings account. You need to study the business' prospects and make sure the managers know what they're doing. This might sound like something that is reserved for wealthy people. Investing in a business does sound a bit intimidating. However, this is what stock market investing is. When you buy shares, you're buying a business. By investing in stocks, you earn what is technically called portfolio income. It's tough to differentiate between passive income and portfolio income clearly. Broadly speaking, the money you receive from your investment activities in the market is called portfolio income. This includes dividends and capital gains.

For the purposes of this book, there isn't much of a difference. In fact, you don't need to understand the differences in great detail in order to make money. The key thing with passive income is that your time spent maintaining and creating the source of income is not connected to how much money you can make from it.

Time Spent Developing Sources

With most passive income streams, you'll need to spend time developing them. A stream such as a savings account doesn't need any time at all to create. However, you'll receive lower sums of money from it. The average savings account barely pays you one percent, and passive income earned at this rate isn't going to move the needle too much. The sources of income that really boost your wealth are stock investments and business investments. When investing in stocks, you have a wide variety of options to choose from. I'll explain these in detail later in this book. When I refer to business investments, these are online businesses that you need to spend time creating. At first, it'll be hard, and you won't make much money in return for the amount of effort you're expending. However, once the income starts rolling in, it'll come in completely independent of how much time you're spending on the business. This is because, with such sources, you'll spend time building traffic up first. Once the traffic is built up to a certain level, your existing customers will refer your business to others, and you'll build momentum. Thus, with very little maintenance, you'll be able to sustain high levels of income. Think of it as a rocket that needs to leave Earth. At first, the rocket burns a ton of fuel to escape Earth's gravity. Once it reaches the upper atmosphere and space, even a small push propels it with high speed due to the lack of friction in space.

Your passive income journey will be the same. The majority of your effort is concentrated in the beginning. Once it gets going, though, you won't have to put in anywhere near the same amount of work into the business. Best of all, the money will keep coming in, and you'll grow your business easily. The key to making successes of such business opportunities is processes. The more reliable and repeatable your process is, the more you can automate it. Automation here refers to having someone else execute your process in return for a fixed amount of money. This way, your business runs itself with minimal input from you, and you earn the lion's share of the money.

This is how you leverage your time. As you read the opportunities in this book, remember that the ultimate aim is to leverage your time and to automate these businesses through rock-solid processes. This applies even to your investments. You should seek the best bang for your buck in terms of time spent on an opportunity.

Benefits of Passive Income

So how does passive income truly benefit you? Some of the advantages are obvious, but it's worth taking the time to understand these advantages in more detail.

More Time

How do you think Bill Gates spends his days? He probably does the things he's most passionate about and spends the rest of his time reading. His wealth is completely disconnected from his time thanks to his investment portfolio, bringing him both cash flow as well as capital gains.

Capital gains are the profits you earn from an investment when you sell it for a higher price. For example, if you buy a stock for $10 and sell it for $20, you've earned a capital gain of $10. Capital gains are mostly unrealized since you don't earn them until you sell your investments.

Cash flow is what you use to pay your bills and your expenses. When looking to generate passive income, it's important that you seek a combination of both. Cash flow pays for your expenses, but truly large gains occur when your investments' value rises.

Either way, the key thing to note is that income earned in this manner frees your time up massively. With more time free, you can create even more streams of income and earn even more money. As more streams automate themselves, you'll have more time on your hands and all the money you can dream of. This is why passive income is so powerful. It gives you more of the one resource you cannot create more of. Time is always running out, no matter what you do. By generating enough money, you create financial freedom, and you can spend your time doing things you truly enjoy.

Reduced Uncertainty

If you have cash coming in from a variety of sources, and if these sources are not correlated with one another, then you'll obviously not have too many worries about the current economy or the state of the world. Sure, you will be concerned, to a certain extent, but you're not going to be one of those people living in fear of what the economy might do tomorrow. I've already mentioned how the world is far more uncertain these days. You cannot rely on the government to protect you or your employer to safeguard your interests. The government is busy printing money to deal with crises, and this only makes things more expensive. The stimulus check you're provided during crises barely pays the rent. The company you work for is busy paying its CEO 100 times more than what you earn, clearly indicating who's more important. You're a resource to be used, and if the cost of employing you is too much, you will be let go. The fact is that if you're relying on a single source of income, you're one step removed from poverty.

The days of a steady job market are long gone. Even if there weren't constant crises to deal with, the rise of automation and robots is guaranteed to wipe out a number of jobs. Consider the field of aerial photography. In the past, you needed a helicopter and a photographer to create aerial videos. These days, anyone can create those images thanks to drones. Self-checkout counters are on the rise, as are automated manufacturing lines. Who's to say your job isn't on the chopping block as well? Build passive income streams as soon as you can, and you won't have to worry about these changes. In fact, you'll put yourself in a position to take advantage of these changes and build even more wealth.

Do What You Love

No one loves reporting on the status of their projects to their bosses. I mean, sure you'll love it if you've done a good job, but does it really get your heart rate pulsing? Would you rather stare at your boss's face, or spend time with your kids? The choice is obvious. Would you rather spend your day cooped up inside an office building, or spend time doing the things that interest you, such as traveling the world or tinkering with your bike?

The standard mindset that people adopt is that they need to sacrifice some of their hobbies to make money and pay for their lives. This is what compromise is, and there's no doubt it's a major part of adult life. However, this doesn't mean you need to compromise all the time. Your objective should be to reduce the number of compromises you accommodate in your life. Compromising with your partner or spouse over an argument is a very different thing from compromising and spending time with your boss in a meeting versus spending time with your family. There are compromises worth making, and those that should be eliminated as much as possible. Passive income helps you get rid of the latter. If you're earning enough money passively to pay for your expenses, do you really need to sit there and listen to your boss's nonsensical plans? Do you need to come in on the weekends in a bid to try and impress them? Do you need to be dependent on their impression of you to get ahead? These questions answer themselves.

Independence

The choice of what to compromise on ties into the theme of independence that passive income generates. You can construct a life that appeals to you the most. If you wish to be location independent and work on the road, then you can do this. If you wish to spend your days gardening and working for just a few hours every day, you can do this as well. These are the things that truly bring us happiness. Most people get caught up in the whirlwind of trying to generate more money and miss the point that money is just a tool. As the popular saying goes, you can't take money with you to your grave. The point is to use money to invest in things that bring you true satisfaction.

To enjoy the things that satisfy you, you need to spend time on them. Time is what you don't have in huge heaps right now. You're busy working a job that brings profits to someone else. You need to prioritize the time you spend at work over the time you spend with your family. In most cases, people chase higher salaries and end up sacrificing their personal time in the process. They justify this choice by pointing out that they could earn more money. What they're really doing is tying themselves even closer to the solitary source of income they have. They're introducing instability into their lives to a greater degree. By making their income even more active and by hoping to save enough of it in the long run, they're increasing their reliance on luck.

Passive income helps you break away from this cycle. Who cares how high up the company's ranks you rise if you're making enough money to buy you enough time to do the things you love? Someone who makes $70,000 per year on their own terms is living a far better life than someone who earns a million dollars from their job but is completely wedded to it. Build your passive income streams now, and you can create more independence in your life instead of relying on someone else to reward you with it.

Stability

All of the above advantages bring you financial stability. More important than stability is the independence that passive income brings. Financial independence is created through passive income generation because you'll have more time to research other income generation ideas. It also gives you the resources needed to test different ideas out. You won't be in a position where a new venture or business "has" to succeed. You can afford to take a few losses. The fact is, to get wealthy, you need to make a few mistakes. You might invest in a property to generate rental returns, but there's no guarantee that this will succeed. If you have a steady cash flow that keeps replenishing your capital, you can spend time testing different business methods out. This, in turn, makes it more likely that you'll land on the business or investment idea that will truly make you money.

What to Avoid

Passive income has become a popular topic, as I've mentioned earlier. There's no shortage of gurus out there promoting passive income to solve all of your problems. As a result, many myths have sprouted, and people who don't understand passive income fall for them. The typical passive income guru charges an exorbitant amount of money for their courses when this information is usually found online for free. There is some benefit to having all of these resources in one place, of course, but this doesn't mean it's worth a ridiculous sum of money.

Here are some of the myths surrounding passive income right now and why they're untrue.

You Don't Need Much Money to Generate Passive Income

This is a pretty common myth. It perpetuates the idea that in order to generate passive income, all you need to do is invest a small amount of money. Passive income is presented as being this windfall of cash that will quickly overtake your active income, and soon, you'll be living on a beach somewhere. There's so much that is untrue to this myth that it's laughable. First, it takes time to build passive income. It probably won't take as long as you think it might, but it'll certainly take longer than what a get rich quick scheme might promise.

Consider the average savings account, which is the easiest way to earn passive income. These accounts pay you one percent a year at best. If your monthly expenses are $2,000, your yearly expenses work out to

$24,000. This means you'll need $2.4 million to generate enough money passively to pay for your expenses. Two million dollars isn't created overnight. It takes time and money to build that much capital. So strap in for the long run. You're not going to create passive income overnight, and you'll need to be patient and steadily increase it over the long run.

You Need a Lot of Money

The previous example has the unintended consequence of discouraging a lot of people from pursuing passive income streams. After all, $2.4 million is a huge amount of money if you're sitting on $10,000 or less in savings. The key is to remove your focus away from the size of the sum you need and to focus instead on supplementing your income every month.

Start off small by investing in savings accounts. If you invest $5,000 into it, you'll get paid $50 every year. This is less than $5 every month. It isn't much at all, but it's something. A lot of passive income and wealth-building sources require far less money than you might think initially. For example, real estate requires money, but there are ways of reducing your upfront expense. If you pursue a traditional mortgage to finance a rental property, you'll need to pay 20% of the price upfront. However, if you pursue a Federal Housing Authority loan, then you can put down just three percent. If the property is worth $100,000, this means you'll need $3,000 plus closing costs to finance the property versus $20,000 plus closing costs. How long will it take you to save $6,000? If you're saving $1,000 per month or can cut your expenses to save this much, you can become a property investor and earn additional cash flow.

My point is that generating passive income requires cash. However, it's important to maintain perspective about how much is needed and tailor your plans accordingly. There is an abundance of business models that can create passive income according to your initial investment ability.

It Requires no Work

You might see ads that claim that a 14-year-old can execute the business model that the guru is promoting to generate passive income. Don't be fooled by such nonsensical claims. Generating passive income of a significant size requires work. You need to spend time creating a framework that will generate income with a high degree of probability. This applies to all forms of passive income generation, whether you're investing in the stock market, real estate, or in your own business. So, don't think of passive income as being something you can set and forget. You'll need to put in the work upfront, as I mentioned earlier, to bring your investment to a stage where it generates enough income for you. Once the investment is up and running, you can afford to take some time away from it. However, don't think that passive income requires no effort or work. This is just unrealistic.

Passive Income Equals "Get Rich Quick"

This myth has come about due to the number of "get rich quick" schemes that use passive income as a marketing tool. The internet has no shortage of charlatans, and you should not make the mistake of thinking passive income is the solution to all of your problems. It can bring about a lot of positive changes in your life, but this doesn't mean you'll achieve these advantages overnight. It takes to build these processes, so be patient. You certainly will not get rich quick.

Passive Income is Easy

The truth is, passive income becomes easier to generate once you gain experience. The first business you start or the first investment you make will probably not pan out. This is understandable since you're doing something for the first time. How good of a driver were you when you first sat behind the wheel of a car? Similarly, it takes time to build expertise in this area. Understanding how passive income works is truly understanding how money works and how wealth is generated. This takes time to learn, and you will make mistakes along the way.

The existence of online businesses makes it seem as if generating passive income is easy. The costs of starting an online business are low, and you don't need any qualifications to do this. If you like designing t-shirts, you might think that generating passive income is as simple as creating a few designs and then selling them through a fulfillment service. However, how do you plan on sending people to your designs? How will you spread the word about them? How do you even know your designs are what people want? Just because you think they're cool doesn't mean your customers do. Are you releasing your designs at a bad time of the year? These are just a few questions surrounding one example of an online side hustle. There will be a lot of other problems and questions you'll need to address before you begin to generate passive income successfully. It isn't easy to generate passive income. But it is rewarding.

I Have to Invest in X, Y or Z

This myth stems from the fact that a few options are the easiest for most people to generate passive income from. For example, the two biggest sources of passive income for most people are the stock market and real estate. Most people think that these are the only ways to generate passive income, and if they aren't invested in them, they don't stand a chance of generating passive income. This is simply not true. The best sources for you are those you can understand, and where you can minimize your risk of losing your investment. Passive income generation isn't something that has just one method attached to it. Just as there are many ways of being successful in life, there are many ways of generating passive income. Take a look around you and see the number of different businesses that exist. This should be a clue as to how many ways exist to make money. With good planning, any of these ways can be turned passive.

Starting a Business is Generating Passive Income

The rise of online businesses has meant that there is an increasing number of avenues you can use to earn money. Online businesses are great in that they lend themselves to automation better than a physical business. However, this doesn't automatically mean that an online business will generate passive income. Most online businesses require you to monitor the associated processes. Besides, you'll have to manage employees remotely, and this will call for a different set of skills. It is possible to generate passive income online, but don't make the mistake of assuming that every online business can do so.

The Mistakes That Beginners Make

Aside from believing the myths previously listed, here are the top 10 mistakes that beginners make. Stay away from these, and you'll manage to avoid a lot of the pitfalls people stumble into when creating passive income.

Skipping Research

This is an extremely important thing to do, and it's something that a lot of beginners underestimate. To have the best chances of success, you need to conduct thorough research into whatever you're investing money in. Beginners get carried away by the idea of passive income generation and think that every idea is foolproof.

The fact is, there are many ways to earn passive income. However, this doesn't mean all of them will be right for you. You need to execute the processes associated with those methods; this is where the money is truly made. So take the time to understand how a particular method works and if you can execute it successfully. This means spending time testing the idea with as little money as possible and measuring your chances of success before going all in and investing in a product or in an opportunity.

Not Creating Processes

To make passive income, you need to create processes that sustain its generation. Too many people approach passive income creation as if it's a one time action, or as if it's easily done. Let's look at a simple example of investing in the stock market.

First, you need to educate yourself about the stock market. You need to understand the various options available to you and how to increase the odds of success. You also have to figure out how much you're willing to risk in the markets and calculate your investment contributions in accordance with your investment goals. All of this takes time to execute. Even after learning all of this, it'll take you some time to put this into practice correctly. Once you do it for the first time, you'll then need to figure out how you can automate your investment. When will you deposit money into your investment accounts, and in what amounts? This is an example of a process that doesn't require you to hire people or have them execute tasks for you. You can see that there are many steps you need to execute. Imagine how much more complex a passive income business will be. The good news is you can learn what you need to do pretty easily. You just need to focus on creating repeatable processes and using the resources that are available to be able to execute them.

Expecting Unrealistic Results

One of the reasons goal setting is hard is because it can be tough to figure out a realistic goal. When it comes to passive income goals, we often underestimate the long term and overestimate the short term. Your goals also depend on the type of plan you're putting into action. If you're planning on creating passive income solely through a savings account, then you can't expect to earn more than one percent on your capital. Expecting a bank to pay you 10% is unrealistic. However, if you're planning on generating money from a business, this is quite conservative.

The key to setting realistic goals is to educate yourself. Talk to people who are already running these businesses, and you'll receive a clear picture of what you can expect. These days, there's a lot of media around online businesses and what results you can expect. Account for the fact that there are fake gurus in every business who will promise you $10,000 in three months. If the offer seems too good to be true, then it probably is. A common tactic scammers and even legitimate online marketers use is to present revenues as profits. They'll tell you they're earning five figures every month, but in reality, this is their revenue figure. Their profits might be less than zero thanks to the amount of money they've spent creating business assets. So, stay away from "get rich quick" sounding schemes and invest your capital wisely.

Not Planning

How much money do you want to earn every month or year, and how long do you think it will take you to earn this amount? Planning well is the key to success since it helps you figure out all the things you need to do to get there. Watching a bunch of YouTube videos and then expecting to really nail a strategy isn't a plan. It's wishful thinking. You might get lucky and execute everything perfectly, but the truth is it takes time for you to obtain results. It's essential for you to plan your passive income methods' execution step by step.

Most people rush right in and invest everything they have into an idea or scheme. This is a mistake. You need to treat everything with skepticism, unless it's a tried and true idea, such as index fund investing (which you'll learn about later in this book.) This is especially the case with online businesses. You need to take the idea out for a trial run before investing more in it. While the method might be a perfectly profitable one, it isn't guaranteed to make you money. This is because your own strengths and weaknesses will exert an influence over the process. So, always plan on testing the waters first with a small investment and then jump in with a larger amount if the plan works in your favor.

Losing Track of Expenditures

In order to make money, you need to spend money. In the rush of thinking you'll earn a ton of money, it's easy to spend a lot of cash on expenses. Even worse, some people try to throw cash at problems with the belief that this will fix everything. This usually increases losses and makes things worse. Just like you track your expenses and income in your personal life using a budget, you need to track business expenses as well. Create spreadsheets that clearly indicate where you've invested your money and where your money is being allocated. Manage your money well, and you'll realize gains from those investments.

Not Managing Assets

Passive income sources need management from time to time. This depends on the asset that creates passive income for you. For example, a savings account doesn't need much maintenance, but a rental property needs maintenance every month. This doesn't make one asset worse than the other; it's just the nature of the beast.

You will need to periodically check in with your assets and make sure everything related to them is running efficiently. Use checklists and task lists to figure out whether this is the case. If a process has been automated electronically, review the workflow. For example, you might have set up an instruction with your bank to transfer 10% of your income to an investment account every month. Has your income changed in the interim? Can you contribute more to get to your goals faster? These kinds of questions should be asked periodically to ensure your assets are performing well for you.

Incurring Fees and Expenses

The easiest way to grow your wealth is to have it compound itself over a long period of time. If you want to hobble yourself and reduce the number of gains you earn from your assets, then make it a point to pay a ton of fees and expenses. This is what a lot of unprofitable investors do when it comes to stock market investment.

Many investors try to get rich quickly and try to time the market through short term trading tactics. These work for some people, but the fact is the odds are overwhelmingly against you. Even worse, trading the markets in this way results in you incurring taxes and brokerage fees, all of which cut into your trading results. The average day trader, someone who times the market's direction to the tune of a few hours or even minutes, needs to earn a 100% return on their money just to breakeven. This is because the fees they incur place such a high barrier to profit. Why would anyone want to make earning money so difficult? Execute your plans in such a way, so you don't pay too many needless fees. Some fees are unavoidable, but look to minimize them as much as possible.

Ignoring Inflation and Taxes

Technically, taxes and inflation are fees and expenses, but it's worth shining the spotlight on them separately. Inflation is a silent wrecker of investment returns. It isn't a cash expense that you incur, and for this reason, most people simply forget about it. Inflation occurs as a normal part of any economy that is healthy. The prices of goods increase over time as an economy grows. This is why a dollar bought a lot more in 1949 than it does today. Currently, inflation is hovering around two to three percent in America. If inflation is costing you two percent every year, then a savings account that pays you one percent every year is actually losing you money. This is why you need to invest your money in places where it can truly grow. Completely passive sources of income do not keep up with inflation, so you should allocate a very small amount of money to them. It's why making passive income is tough; you need to teach yourself new skills and execute processes.

Taxes can be minimized, but not eliminated completely. The best way of minimizing taxes is to invest for the long term. The longer you hold onto your investment, the lesser the government taxes you. In fact, you could get away with paying zero taxes if you invest long enough. After all, you'll incur capital gains taxes only when you sell. If you never sell, there are no taxes for you to pay.

Being Cheap

While you need to minimize expenses, don't minimize them for the sake of doing so. What will happen is that you'll end up creating an inferior asset. Imagine you own a car and now need someone to maintain it. Would you choose a mechanic solely based on price, or would you go to the person who has the best skills? While price does play a role, it isn't the only factor in the decision-making process. Evaluate everything based on the benefits they bring you and act accordingly. This is why you should minimize expenses, not eliminate them.

Buying Something You Don't Understand

The "get rich quick" attitude convinces you that you need to invest your money into the latest thing, or else you're going to miss out on easy money. This leads to a person investing in everything under the sun, and the result is a string of failed ventures. Instead, try to understand the business model or investment plan before sinking money into it. If you don't understand it, it isn't a missed opportunity. It's a bit like not understanding someone who speaks a foreign language. If they were asking you for water and you didn't understand them and walked right past, does this mean you're a bad person? Hardly!

Similarly, if you don't understand a business or investment idea, how can you miss out on it if you don't invest? Stick to the things you know and educate yourself as much as possible on how things work. This way, you'll increase your field of knowledge and can expand your investments.

Chapter 2:

The Investor's Mindset

To accomplish something, you need to have the right mindset for it. Your mind is the most powerful tool in the world, but unfortunately, we overload it with all kinds of unnecessary baggage. We absorb beliefs from those around us and believe in things that are completely immaterial to us. We distract ourselves and consume information that has no bearing on our future or on our wellbeing. How often do you read political news and get outraged at what's happening in the country? How often do you keep yourself up to date with the stock market and become euphoric or consumed by fear?

There's a lot of information thrown at you on a daily basis, and your task is to be vigilant in allowing what enters your mind. Only absorb the things that help you and reject those that harm you. To be successful as an investor of passive income, you need to master four tools of thinking. You can view them as being components of an overall mindset or as individual qualities:

- Determination
- Organization
- Motivation
- Goal orientation

Determination

Determination is a state of mind where your focus and energy is pointed towards one particular goal or outcome. Determination can be thought of as being a higher state of intentionality. If your intention defines what you wish to achieve through your actions, then determination is what ramps it up to a higher degree. The great thing is that determination is a skill that can be learned by anyone. All it takes is practice. In fact, all of the four skills of the investing mindset can be learned through practice. Practicing determination is as easy as repeating the habits of determined people. Here are the five traits of highly determined people and how you can emulate them.

Know Your Strengths

Everyone has certain strengths and weaknesses. It's impossible for a person to be successful at everything they do, no matter what it looks like on the outside. The thing that highly successful people have figured out is that they realize they can only win the games they understand. For example, you won't find a basketball player trying his hand at baseball or football. A supreme athlete like Michael Jordan did, and even he failed at baseball. The point is that in order to succeed, you need to play games you can win. Investing in things you understand is an outcome of this mindset.

You cannot hope to master everything at once, so take your time figuring out which investment method matches your skills. Some people are great at figuring out online businesses, while others prefer to invest in real estate. There's no wrong answer here. It depends entirely on you. This is why I highlighted the myth about having to invest in certain things previously. This is wrong because no one is good at everything. You can certainly learn new skills and become good at them. However, to hope to master everything at once is unrealistic. So take an inventory of your strengths and carry out your processes in line with them.

If you're someone who struggles to think creatively and on a large scale, perhaps trying to set up a large business is unrealistic. Instead, you can execute more technical processes that depend on the details. Act in line with your strengths, and you'll find that your ability to remain determined will increase. This is because you're acting in alignment with who you are and aren't trying to win games you have no skills at. You only have a finite amount of energy to dedicate to a task, so dedicate it to something you know you have a good chance of winning.

Find Your Purpose

Without getting too spiritual on you, attaining success is so much easier when your actions are aligned with who you want to be. Everyone has a purpose in life that they want to achieve. Unfortunately, most of us are blind to it and end up working on things that mean nothing to us. Some people get lucky and end up working on what truly moves them right from the beginning. Others stumble into it by accident. For most of us, we need to figure out what we truly want to do with our lives. This is not an easy task. Many things suggest themselves to us, and it can be tough to try to execute everything. It's far easier, instead, to ask yourself what you don't want to do with your life and work from there.

By eliminating the scenarios that definitely do not appeal to you, you'll be able to narrow your options down to a more manageable size. From that, you'll find it easier to figure out what it is you truly want.

Determination and willpower are a lot easier to summon when you're truly engaged with what you're doing. How many times have you been caught up in a task and forgotten how quickly time slips by? There's no better motivator in life than your purpose. Get in alignment with it, and you'll notice how easy things become. Take the time to visualize what kind of life you want. Define everything about it, or as much as you can. Work backward from there. How much money will it cost, and how long will it realistically take to earn that much? Don't worry about how you're going to achieve that life. Simply focus on working backward and figure out the numbers.

Once you have the numbers mapped out roughly, ask yourself how you can achieve them. Perhaps it involves learning new skills or creating a new investment path. Work on those processes one by one, and you'll get there. If this sounds simple, it's because it is. We complicate things by imposing our emotions and expectations on these tasks and end up derailing ourselves.

Practice Delayed Gratification

In 1965, a scientist at Stanford University conducted a simple test. His name was Water Mischel, and his objective was to measure the degree of self-control children had (Clear, 2014). To measure this, he created a situation where a child was asked to sit on a table. In front of the child was a piece of candy or a marshmallow. The child was told that if he or she could resist eating it for 15 minutes, they would be rewarded with another treat that they could enjoy freely. Some children were able to resist temptation and used any means necessary. Some deliberately looked away from the marshmallow while some sat on their hands. Others hummed or made noises to distract themselves while some chewed paper. Another portion of kids couldn't resist and ended up eating the marshmallow.

Mischel and his team collected these results and published them. The interesting thing about this experiment occurred two decades later. In the 1980s, Mischel happened to get back in touch with his original subjects out of curiosity. They were now fully grown adults, with the youngest among them in the first year of college. He noticed a fascinating pattern. The kids who were able to resist temptation seemed to have better careers and had higher SAT scores than the ones who didn't. Mischel dug deeper into the data and conducted more detailed interviews, and this pattern held up. The kids who could delay gratification uniformly achieved more success in life, when measured by standard metrics.

Delayed gratification is a superpower when it comes to your personal life. It doesn't mean you need to deny yourself life's pleasures, but it helps you make decisions with a clear head. The marshmallow experiment proves this as a fact. Here's a little exercise you should conduct with your spending. The next time you want to spend money on something that isn't strictly necessary, wait for a week. If you find that you still want it after a week, go ahead and buy it. If you find your enthusiasm dimmed, then don't buy it. This simple technique will save you a ton of money since we're emotional beings. It's tough to resist their call in the moment. However, success comes to those who manage their emotions well. Build your well of determination by resisting these short term urges, and you'll set yourself up for success.

Believe

Believe in yourself and your mission. The world is full of naysayers, and you will be questioned every step of the way. Build the ability to absorb feedback but to not be emotionally swayed by it. The extent to which you can entertain contrary feedback and still execute your plans is a mark of how successful you'll be.

Warren Buffett, the billionaire investor, is a great example of this. During the early apportion of his career, he would understand everything he could about a company he was looking to invest in and would then pitch this idea to his friend Charlie Munger (Schroeder, 2009). Munger, given his disposition, would dissect and rip the idea to shreds. He'd point out the numerous ways everything could go wrong and the risks associated with it. Buffett would listen and absorb all of Munger's points. Once he'd considered everything, he would inform

Munger whether he was going to go ahead with his plan or not. Munger would do the same thing with Buffett, and eventually, the two of them decided to partner up in business. This habit of theirs was borrowed from Charles Darwin, who would rigorously argue the opposite point of his arguments in his head and draw conclusions appropriately.

Most of us get emotionally wedded to our ideas, and as a result, we move away from facts. When someone challenges our assumptions, we react emotionally and strengthen our biases. Instead, be open to questioning and ask yourself whether you've truly considered all your plan's weaknesses. Every plan has a weakness. Your task is to mitigate it through your processes. It takes a while to develop this kind of thought process. It's a product of believing in your ability to handle tough situations and emerge stronger. This is what will make you money in the long run.

Stay Healthy

Without your health, you'll have nothing. You could be the world's wealthiest person, but it's of no use if you're bed-ridden or constantly anxious, thanks to stress. Our world is full of stress these days, so work to reduce it as much as possible. Don't overwork yourself in the name of being determined or hard working. Sometimes, the best thing to do is to do nothing. Relax and take a nap. You're not being lazy, you're being kind to yourself. Don't compare your work habits to someone else's. Instead, be honest with yourself about the amount of work you can get done and execute your tasks appropriately.

Organization

Being organized is one of the pillars of success. The mistake that people make is thinking that organization looks the same at all times. Just as different people have different talents, so their methods of organization vary. For example, the famous French playwright, Gaston Leroux, would fire his pistol into the ceiling when he was done with a particularly tough piece of drama or before he started writing. Winston Churchill would sip a weak whiskey and soda around 5 P.M every day and nap for two hours. This allowed him to get through a day and half's worth of work within a single day. Nikola Tesla napped for 20 minutes every hour and got by with just two hours of sleep every 24 hours using this method. You don't need to fire guns in the air or adopt bizarre sleep schedules to be successful. Instead, you need to do what works for you. Don't seek to copy what others do. Emulate them by figuring out what works best for you instead. Being organized makes you more productive by freeing up your time.

Remember how time is the one resource that you can never create more of? Well, being productive allows you to squeeze more out of your time and generate a greater return on investment (ROI.) Since you'll have more time to get things done, you'll be able to reduce the stress you experience. This, in turn, will deliver massive boosts to your health. Disorganized environments tend to create clutter within our minds. How often have you walked into a dirty and cluttered space and have experienced a block in your creativity? This is because a cluttered environment increases stress within us, and we cannot truly be our best selves. So if you're experiencing any blocks in your creativity, start by decluttering your immediate environment.

Your goals will also receive a boost due to you finding the things you need and executing your processes easily. Thanks to the combined effects of reduced stress, better health, more creativity and better organization, you'll easily hit your goal deadlines. This, in turn, boosts your energy and you'll set better goals and work with a better frame of mind. Organization also helps you declutter your workspace, and this will help you remain in a better state of mind. The net result of all of these advantages is that you'll end up making more money, which is the goal after all.

Here are some of the best methods of getting organized.

Plan Your Day

I'm not talking about writing a to-do list and leaving it at that. I'm talking about planning each and every minute of your day in advance the night before. Create time blocks for work tasks and adhere to them. If you happen to work in a creative field or one that requires intense concentration, work in blocks of 25 minutes and then take a five-minute break at the end of it. This work technique is called the Pomodoro technique, and it helps your brain retain more information. Apply this method when you read books as well. You'll find that by reviewing the information you just read in the five minute rest period, you'll manage to retain more information.

When scheduling your day ahead of time, keep in mind that there will be tasks that will spill over and you'll have to deal with unexpected interruptions. This is fine. The point isn't to strictly adhere to the schedule you created. Planning your day ahead of time will boost your productivity all by itself. This is because it forces you to think of how you execute your tasks, and how much rest you need between them. When working in a disorganized fashion, you might end up taking longer breaks than intended, and this cuts into the work hours you have. Design your work blocks to have some spillage. This could be 15 minutes long or more, depending on the task. The point is to think deeply about your work and how you execute your tasks. It primes your brain for execution, and you'll find that you can complete your tasks much more efficiently.

90-90-1

This productivity rule is espoused by the leadership coach Robin Sharma. The rule is quite simple. For the next 90 days, devote the first 90 minutes of your workday to the single best opportunity you currently have. All of us have big dreams within us, but finding the time to execute it is tough. We have regular jobs and demands on our time from family, friends, etc. What often stops us from chasing our big dreams is fear. Fear is a natural emotion to feel when chasing huge goals. The problem occurs when we give in to the fear and use regular events in our lives as distractions to avoid pursuing the big goal. This work method eliminates that possibility. It's quite simple to execute, and its beauty lies in its simplicity. You might not have 90 minutes upon waking up. However, you can make time for it by waking up earlier.

There are different variations of this rule that you can implement. You can work on your huge goal or dream for even 15 minutes upon waking up. This isn't such a daunting task. Anyone can wake up half an hour earlier and get to work on their project. You could even set aside another 15 minutes to work on it in the evenings. This way, you'll be working on it for 30 minutes every day. This might not sound like much, but keep in mind that consistency is what builds results. Show up every day and keep doing what needs to be done. Your efforts will compound, and you'll end up creating outsized results in your life.

When executing the important tasks, focus on doing what's in front of you. It's easy to get lost in the "how am I going to do that?" mode of thinking with big goals. The point of a huge and ambitious goal is that you'll have no idea how to get there. Think of it as standing at the base of Everest and trying to look at the peak. It's impossible. Instead, focus on taking one step at a time. Refine your execution and repeat it. Step by step, you'll learn more about what works, and you'll get there. If you allow yourself to get lost in the execution of each step, you'll feel as if you got to the peak in no time. The problem occurs when you keep trying to look at the peak. This action will remind you of how far away you are, and no one can work with the negativity in place. It's a bit like an athlete looking at the scoreboard when playing. There's no way they can focus on the task in front of them.

Implement the Pareto Principle

The Pareto principle is also called the 80/20 rule, and it states that 80% of our results come from 20% of tasks, and 20% of results come from 80% of tasks. This is an extremely powerful rule to adopt when it comes to executing your plans and goals. Consider a task that you engage in daily, such as driving your vehicle. What are the things that ensure you're safe on the road, above all else? Here's a rough list:

- Checking your vehicle is in a safe condition
- Remaining alert and watching your mirrors
- Driving at a safe speed

Executing these things will pretty much guarantee you'll arrive at your destination safely, barring anything unexpected happening. There are a few other driving tips that keep you safe apart from these three things:

- Holding the steering wheel correctly
- Maintaining two car lengths between you and the person ahead (tough to do in cities)

- Checking your blind spots regularly even when traveling in a straight line
- Wearing comfortable driving shoes so that your feet don't get fatigued
- Not eating in your car since food might distract you
- Making sure you're seated comfortably and that your seat cushions you well
- Allowing your car manufacturer to track your movements in case an emergency occurs

Notice that the first list is way more important than the second list. If you execute those three things, you'll get there safely more often than not. Execute the second list without paying attention to the first, and there's no guarantee you'll arrive safely. For example, you could be seated comfortably and check your blind spots like a hawk, but if you're driving at 120 constantly, you're more likely than not going to end up in an accident. Similarly, you could do everything correctly but if your vehicle isn't in a condition to safely bring you home (brakes, lights, indicators etc.) all of your actions are for naught.

The Pareto principle makes us aware of the most important things when executing a task. Do these basic things, and you obtain 80% or more of your desired result. You can apply this to pretty much anything. To dress well, you need to be well-groomed and wear clothes that fit you and aren't shabby looking. That's pretty much all there is to it. You could choose to wear clothes of a certain cut, style or fashion but these are accessory tasks. They don't deliver the majority of your results by themselves. The great thing about working this way is that it frees up your mental cognition. By focusing on just a few tasks, you can devote mental resources to other important tasks, and you'll be less stressed. After all, you don't need to execute a mountain of tasks. All you need to execute are a few things, and you'll be good to go!

Motivation

Motivation is a prime topic when it comes to self-help books. The truth is that a lot of people struggle with motivation. They think they aren't motivated enough or are too lazy when this happens, and end up sabotaging themselves. The problem isn't with getting motivated. The problem is with their thinking. If you're suffering from a lack of motivation, you're not setting big enough goals, or your goals just don't mean anything to you. This is why it's important for you to begin with the "why" behind your goal. If you don't know why your goal exists, or what it means to you, you're going to lack motivation.

The biggest reason for the lack of motivation is that your current actions do not align with your purpose. Finding your purpose doesn't require you to travel to a forest and meditate under a sacred tree (although that can't hurt). It's as simple as doing the things you enjoy doing. You might be complicating the process of finding your purpose by overthinking and focusing on the lack of purpose. For example, you might be thinking that you can't seem to find a purpose, and might be trying extremely hard to find something. This is focusing on the lack of a purpose. Instead, relax and do the things that appeal to you in the present moment. For example, you might be wanting to take a walk. Go ahead and do it. It sounds trivial to say such things, but you'll only find your purpose when you begin listening to yourself. Most of us can't do this. Instead, we listen to what the world tells us to do and how to behave. Getting back in touch with yourself will help you move closer to who you really are and your purpose will illuminate itself.

Once you move closer to your purpose, you'll find that motivation is no problem. Think back to a time when you lost track of time and remained focused on something. It could have occurred when you were watching a movie or your favorite TV show. You probably got lost in the moment, and time seemed to stretch forever. Once the movie ended, you probably wondered how time passed by so quickly. You had no problem motivating yourself to watch this movie.

So, why do you have a problem when it comes to your work tasks? It's just because the task isn't stimulating your brain enough. You'll stimulate your brain when you do the things it loves doing, which is another way of saying you need to find your purpose. Sit down right now and write out all the things you want to do in your life, assuming resources were not a factor. Where do you want to go, how much money do you want to make and how do you want to live? Write all of these things down. Now take a look at your list and see if there's anything you can do right now or within a short period of time. Check these off your list and do them. You'll find that once you finish doing these things, your mind will generate new ideas as to how you can achieve some of the more complicated things on your list. Slowly but surely, you'll begin taking steps to execute them. As you keep plotting your way forward, you'll also become attuned to why these goals are important to you.

Perhaps they improve your quality of living, or perhaps they'll result in your family gaining something. But, when you combine your purpose with your "why," you'll have no motivation problems whatsoever. In fact, your challenge will be to listen to yourself and take rest when you need to. You'll be so pumped up to work that you'll forget to keep track of time. This doesn't mean you won't get down on yourself and that you won't have tough times. These are inevitable if you're alive. It's better to face challenges and difficulties related to your purpose instead of facing them in things you have no interest in.

Give Your Ideas a Chance

Failure is inevitable. I'm not talking about you failing at your bigger goal. I'm talking about you encountering seemingly impossible difficulties. It's normal to feel discouraged and to feel deflated during such times. It's important to remain kind towards yourself in such moments and remind yourself that your ideas are worthy. The key is to reframe what failure is. We've been conditioned since childhood to be scared of failure. We do our best to shy away from it and avoid it. Think back to your school days when you were afraid of giving the wrong answer to your teacher's question. This attitude carries over into adulthood, and we shy away from doing tough things. However, failure is how we learn. True failure is when you don't even try or take action.

Anyone who takes action towards achieving their goal can never be a failure no matter what their results are like.

Build Anticipation

A key component of being successful is to get excited. Think back to your childhood and how you felt on Christmas Eve. You knew something special would be waiting for you when you woke up the next day, and you probably couldn't sleep at night. Why did you feel like this? It probably had to do with the fact that you were 100% certain that there would be a gift waiting for you. Why not approach your goals in the same manner? When you were a kid, you couldn't see your parents buying you a gift or wrapping it. You just knew and trusted that it would be there. Why not do this as an adult with your goals? As adults, we demand all kinds of things, such as evidence and practicality when it comes to our goals. We don't trust ourselves and the process. As a result, the thing we want doesn't occur for the most part. So get excited and look forward to achieving your goals. Know that it's already there. You just need to move towards it.

Start Small

If you're unaccustomed to setting goals and acting in accordance with your purpose, then start small. It doesn't make sense to set out after a huge goal right off the bat. This will only scare you away and will end your motivation, causing damage. This is why I suggested you begin by listening to what you want to do right now. Let everything else fall into place. If you act according to who you are, you'll find that your goals and dreams will become achievable.

Get Support

No one can do everything by themselves. It's important for you to recruit support for yourself. Confide in those you trust and seek their help. If they're truly close to you, they'll help you achieve your goals. Most people who seek ambitious goals are guilty of trying to do everything by themselves. Take a step back and seek support. Learn to delegate tasks to those who can help you achieve your goals. You'll find your journey that much more enjoyable.

Focus on the Benefits

It's easy to get lost in the size of your goal and start wondering how on Earth you'll achieve what you want. This is to focus on the problem and not on the benefits. One of the things that really push you towards your goal is to focus on the benefits of achieving the goal. How will you feel when you achieve your goal? Close your eyes and visualize this. Feel the emotion. Think of all the good things that achieving your goal will bring. Now open your eyes and get back to work (if you feel the need.)

Goal Oriented Mindset

A common attribute that successful people share is that all of them are goal-oriented or solution-oriented. This is in stark contrast to the average person who is problem-oriented. The minute an obstacle is encountered, the solution-oriented person swings into action and tries to uncover ways to make the situation better. Don't mistake this attitude for one which ignores the problem and carries on as if nothing is the matter. That's just being delusional.

A solution-oriented mindset considers the present problems and works to reduce the issue as much as possible. This mindset recognizes that problems occur, but as long as a person keeps striving to find solutions, they'll happen at some point, and the problem will be taken care of. A negative mindset focuses on the problem itself and on how it makes the person feel. For example, if you happen to have a flat tire on the way to an important meeting, how would you react? Understand that the successful person will also curse their luck and let out a string of expletives. However, they'll quickly weigh their options and jump into action.

An unsuccessful person will begin telling themselves how the universe is against them and that they have no hope of success and so on. The same even thus creates two completely different points of focus. The degree with which you're able to orient yourself towards your goals and solutions will determine your level of success. Thinking in this manner requires practice. You need to repeat this thought process over and over until it becomes second nature to you. Unfortunately, there's no shortcut to this. There is no plug and play solution when it comes to learning. You'll need to train yourself to develop this attitude.

The good news is that this attitude is a habit like everything else. Repeat it often enough, and it will become as automatic as brushing your teeth is for you. Solution-oriented mindset is so powerful because it places your focus on the positive aspects of the situation. By refocusing away from the negative, you change your energy. This is necessary if your aim is to earn passive income. There are different methods of earning this, and each method has its pros and cons. You need to be able to evaluate each method with respect to your own abilities and figure out what works best for you. Often, you'll need to test passive income streams before you put them into action fully. For example, a new business idea will need to be thoroughly tested before you put it into action. This will cost you money. You might end up testing a ton of business ideas unsuccessfully before you hit the one idea that works best for you.

Throughout this process, you will need to focus on that single idea that will make you money. Thomas Edison famously quipped that he didn't fail thousands of times. He simply learned what didn't work that many times before finding the one way that did. This is a great illustration of how a goal-oriented mindset works. Keep looking forward to finding the solution to your problems, and you'll end up creating wealth and prosperity as a side effect. Regarding passive income, it's important for you to define a few things ahead of time since these will stand you in good stead in the long run.

Conduct a Personal Inventory

I'm not talking about an inventory of your possessions. I'm talking about what's within your head. What kinds of attitudes and beliefs are you carrying within you that will sabotage your progress towards your goals? How aware of them are you, and what steps are you taking to destroy them? Set aside time every day to take action towards reducing the negative impact of these limiting beliefs. Ask yourself what your beliefs surrounding money look like and how they've been limiting you. Implement plans that will help you install habits that reduce their impact. Repeat these actions daily, and you'll manage to make progress before you know it.

Time and Money

What is your passive income goal? How much money do you want to earn every month, and by when do you want this to occur? Goal setting is important, as you already know. Setting a time-oriented goal is important because it helps build urgency and motivate you to work hard and start executing tasks successfully.

Everyone has different types of goals. Some people want to earn a certain amount of money, while others want a certain amount of cash flow every month. Whatever your goals are, they're yours, so don't judge them. You don't need to share them with anyone, and they're no one's business but yours. You want to set realistic targets to achieve your goals. For example, if you're earning $2,000 per month right now and want to earn $10,000 every month, you're talking about increasing your income five times. This is not going to happen overnight. At the very least, it could take you a year. Break down that goal into further sub-goals. For example, to earn $10,000, you need at least two income streams. That's the point of passive income, after all. What will these income streams look like, and how will you build them? Create a vision for your goals. A vision is a roadmap that will take you towards your goals, and you'll be able to map your progress as you travel along your path. It tells you what's next and you can plan what to do to get there.

Research

Research is something you'll need to do every step of the way. You're trying to create something that doesn't exist, so you'll need to figure out how to get there with what you have. You'll have to create solutions where none exist, and this calls for creativity. Even if you think you aren't a creative person, thorough research will help you figure out how to get from A to B. You don't need to reinvent the wheel. You just need to design one that fits your needs. Research can be conducted by reading reviews, watching informational videos, and so on. You'll also encounter a lot of fake reviews and research that will try to mislead you. It's just the nature of the internet these days. So take the time to become aware of your weaknesses and learn to spot the marketing ploys that trigger those weaknesses in you. Develop the attitudes of determination, goal orientation, organization, and motivation within you, and you'll come a lot closer to making your passive income dreams a reality.

Chapter 3:

Passive Investing

One of the best ways to generate passive income is through intelligent passive investing. Passive Investing refers to automated investment strategies that you can set and forget. This approach has a number of benefits that you will learn about later in this chapter. For now, let's dive in and take a look at what passive investing is and why it's so powerful. The average person believes that successful stock market investing is all about unearthing some special opportunity in the markets and finding some kind of a secret key to unlock market secrets. This is pretty much how professional money managers operate. They recruit armies of researchers and analysts to find opportunities that they can invest in. They then run these opportunities through their investment screening criteria and focus on the ones that pass the test. This way, their time is used efficiently, and they don't need to worry about constantly generating new ideas.

The average investor who adopts this approach thus faces formidable competition. If your aim is to find stocks and companies that are undiscovered gold mines, you're going to have to devote a lot of time to analyze the markets. It's far from impossible to succeed, but it's going to be tough. People who don't work for investment institutions or investment funds have full-time jobs that take up a significant portion of their day. You're probably one of these people. You don't have eight hours a day to devote to market and company research. You have at most two hours every day and need to make the best use of this time. Within these two hours, you'll also be focused on creating another passive income stream, such as a side hustle. Thus, the average person is best served by following a passive investing strategy. What if you could spend just two hours every week analyzing the best opportunities and allocate money towards them?

What if these opportunities would then go away and keep making you money non-stop? All you'd have to do is then keep allocating money to them in periodic intervals, and your investing is all taken care of? Sounds too good to be true? Well, this strategy is being followed by millions of investors around the world and has existed since the markets have existed. The reason many people don't follow a passive strategy is that it's too simple. We tend to complicate things in a bid to feel smart or intelligent. We don't realize that simplicity is often the best way of making money or creating value. Warren Buffett is often asked why so many people fail at stock market investing, and his reply is that everyone wants to get rich quickly, but no one wants to get rich slowly. Passive investing takes time to pay you results, but the flip side is that the results are virtually guaranteed. To understand how a passive investing strategy works, you need to first understand a few basics about the market.

Dividends

You've already learned that a single share represents a piece of a company. Companies engage in businesses that produce profits and losses for them yearly. There are two kinds of companies that exist: Private and public. Very few people are sole owners of private companies, and their shares are not available for public purchase. Public companies are the ones that trade on the stock exchange, and anyone can buy shares in them. When investing passively, you'll be focusing on public companies. This is because public companies have to follow a strict set of rules when it comes to disclosures and reporting standards. These companies' activities in the market are regulated by the Securities and Exchange Commission (SEC). They file an annual report called the 10-K in addition to a host of other filings surrounding the actions of the company management and owners. All of these filings are available for free from the SEC's website.

Given that a share represents ownership in the business, it stands to reason that shareholders are entitled to a cut of the company's profits in proportion to their ownership share. This is true; however, in practice, it doesn't always work that way. For starters, shareholders can claim a portion of profits, but it might not be in the company's best interests to pay these profits out in cash. Such cash distributions are called dividends. Companies don't pay dividends because their businesses need cash to sustain themselves. For example, Facebook doesn't pay dividends because it's in an extremely competitive sector. It has to constantly have cash on hand to purchase new technologies and companies that can potentially overtake it. It needs cash to reinvest and improve its platform. If it were to pay out its profits in dividends, then this would harm the business.

Companies that are growing quickly and are operating in tough sectors usually don't pay dividends. In contrast, companies that have achieved a dominant position in their business and generate enough cash to take care of reinvestment needs to pay a dividend. More often than not, these are mature companies that don't have their founders on board anymore. For example, Coca Cola has been in existence forever and has such a dominant position in the market that they generate cash over and above what their business needs to maintain itself. Thus, the company has not only paid its shareholders a dividend for over 50 years; it's constantly increased the dividend amount that it has paid over that time. Another example of such a company is Kimberly Clark. You've probably never heard of it, but you've probably used one of its brands, such as Huggies, Scott, and Cottonelle. The company is in the business of manufacturing household paper products and has been around forever. It is also a company that has increased its dividend constantly over the past 50 years.

Investing in these companies is like investing in a savings account. They're likely going to be around for a long time, and their dividends are effectively interest payments on your investment. While they aren't as safe as savings accounts, their lengthy track records and uncomplicated business structures make them as close to savings accounts as possible. However, there is a risk that these companies might go under. After all, nothing is guaranteed, and who can say what the future will bring? People might move away from Coca Cola's high fructose corn syrup concoctions and choose healthier alternatives thereby decreasing its advantage. This risk exists when investing in any individual company. The company could go bankrupt or, even worse, remain stationary for a long period and not give any return on your investment. To discover the true extent of risk in your investment, you need to spend a lot of time studying the markets, and this isn't available to everyone. So what should the average investor do? Is there anything they can do to ensure their money always earns a return and in a safe manner? It turns out there is.

Indexes

Stock market performance is often traced through an index. In America, the most famous index is the Standard & Poor's 500 or S&P 500. This index was created to capture the mightiest companies in America and their performance. It lists the 500 largest companies trading on public stock exchanges and tracks their stock prices. The stock prices of these companies are averaged, and this gives the index its value. Thus, by looking at the index's value, an investor can instantly know how the market has been performing. Indexes are fantastic for one particular reason. As long as America's economy continues to grow and sustain itself, indexes will rise in value over the long term. This is because America's economy is composed of companies. Companies that do well will grow in size, and the economy benefits.

As companies grow in size, older ones will grow unprofitable. For example, Sears was once a part of the S&P 500. In case you don't know what Sears was, it was a department store giant. It went bankrupt a few years earlier and doesn't trade anymore. However, the fall of Sears didn't impact the value of the S&P 500 index. This is because as Sears' performance began declining, it was screened out of the index. In its place technology companies, such as Google, Facebook, and Amazon were screened in. As far as the index is concerned, the individual performance of the companies in it is immaterial. If one falls out, another company that satisfies the criteria is screened in. Thus, the index manages to capture the best of the best, no matter what. There is a downside to the index. Its value will never rise as high as the best performing stock within it. For example, Amazon might climb to stratospheric heights, but since the stock is just one portion of a large number of stocks in the index, the index's value will not rise as high. The index will always capture the average performance of the stocks contained within it. It's the very definition of getting rich slowly. You cannot expect its value to shoot upwards instantly overnight or expect it to grow by 20% every year. You can expect it to be worth whatever the average value of its underlying stocks is.

Indexes can be created for pretty much any criteria you can think of. If you want to create an index of stocks in the biotech sector whose names begin with "A," you're welcome to do so. Whether anyone will follow this index or whether it'll have any credibility is up for debate. The best indexes are issued or created by reputable corporations. Some of the most popular and well-respected indexes are issued by companies such as Standard & Poor's, Moody's, iShares, and Barclay's. There are smaller indexes as well, but these companies dominate the space. The key thing that drives index performance is its criteria. Some indexes capture the performance of dividend stocks to varying degrees. For example, the Dividend Aristocrats index consists of companies that have increased their dividends for at least 25 years. The Dividend Achievers index consists of companies that have increased their dividends for at least 10 years.

If you're following along this far, you'll realize that investing in the index itself will be quite profitable. After all, it's an instrument designed to go up over time (assuming the economy does) and automatically screens in the best-performing stocks all by itself. The problem is that an index is not a tradable instrument. It's a snapshot of the market and thus can't be bought or sold. This doesn't mean your plans are dead in the water, though. You can still capture the magic of indexes in your portfolio. You can do this manually or automatically.

The manual method involves buying and selling all of the securities in the index, and maintaining these securities in the same proportion as in the main index. The positive aspect of this method is that you can capture index performance for free, and you'll only have to look at the stocks in the index to figure out what to buy and sell. The negative is that you'll have to constantly track the index for changes. Also, if the index changes in proportions a lot, you'll constantly have to buy and sell stocks. Lastly, if your capital is small, you won't likely be able to execute this strategy since you won't be able to buy fractional shares in companies. This is where the automated method of investing comes into play.

Index Dividend Investing

Instead of manually buying and selling all stocks in the dividend indexes, you can simply buy an exchange traded fund (ETF) or an index fund that mimics the index's movement. Here's how they work. The ETF or index fund has a manager whose sole job is to carry out this tracking. They buy and sell stocks in the index and construct their own portfolio to match the index. Since the fund's assets are large, they can do this effectively. In fact, most index ETFs and funds use robots to correctly calculate portfolio percentages and create optimized portfolios. As an investor, all you have to do is buy a unit of these funds, and you'll attain all of the performance that the index provides. Mind you, it might decline in the short term and might be depressed for a few years. However, in the long run, the American stock market has returned 10% compounded every year on average (*S&P 500 Historical Annual Returns*, 2009). This means, as long as your holding period is for over a decade or two, you will most likely earn these kinds of returns. All you need to do is remain invested and keep contributing to your investment every year. How much you contribute depends on your goals.

Let's say you're 30 years old right now and want to own a million-dollar portfolio by the age of 50. How much should you contribute to your ETF portfolio? Let's assume the market will grow at an average rate of 10% every year. To reach one million, you need to contribute roughly $17,500 every year to your ETF portfolio. That's $1,500 every month. What if you can't contribute this much? Well, this is where creating multiple income streams comes into play. However, suppose you can contribute this amount of money. In that case, all you need to do is set it aside, and you'll almost certainly be a millionaire. It's impossible not to succeed at getting rich slowly, as you can see. This isn't a sexy strategy, and it's not going to get pulses racing. However, it works. In exchange for having the ETF manager take care of your portfolio, you'll need to pay a management fee. This is usually less than 0.05% of your invested principal in index funds and ETFs.

The best part of this strategy is that you can tailor it to pretty much any type of investment strategy you like. If you think tech stocks will dominate over the next 50 years, buy an ETF that tracks an index of tech stocks. If you think utilities are always going to be around thanks to constant demand, buy an ETF that tracks them. I've proposed investing in dividends because these companies are stable, and your portfolio is guaranteed to return a certain amount every year thanks to the dividends that you will be paid. Let's look at some of the advantages of investing in dividends.

Advantages of Dividend Investing

The biggest advantage that dividends give you is that they allow you to earn cash and capital gains on your investments. They're like a piece of property that you've placed on rent. You benefit by earning from the rise in the property's value and the rental cash flow that your tenants bring. Stock dividends usually yield around two to three percent. The yield is calculated by dividing the annual dividend payment by the price you paid for the stock. For example, if you get paid a dividend of $2 on a stock purchase of $100, your yield is two percent. Two percent doesn't sound like much but, your compounding receives a boost when you begin reinvesting those dividends.

Reinvestment

All brokers offer you the option of reinvesting your dividends in the security you received it from. If a stock pays you $2 every year, you can use this money to buy more stock. These plans are called dividend reinvestment programs or DRIPs. The biggest advantage that DRIPs offer is that they allow you to buy fractional shares in the security. From the previous example, you can buy $2 worth of a $100 stock. If you elect to receive the dividends as cash and then try to purchase the stock, you won't be able to buy fractional shares. Thus, DRIPs fully automate your investment process.

Remember, the goal of passive income is to automate your money flow as much as possible. This is how you disconnect your earning ability from your time spent creating it. Opt for a DRIP, and you'll create a dividend snowball that keeps increasing as the years go by. When allied with your monthly purchases of stock or units in the ETF, you'll see that your dividends will soon begin amounting to a serious amount of money every year. By reinvesting them back in, you'll create a situation where they compound, thereby boosting your gains even more.

Stability

Dividend investing is boring. I say that in the most positive sense possible. The companies that pay dividends don't have CEOs who go on Twitter to drum up publicity for their companies. They're not "disrupting" anything, nor are they trying to give humanity a backup plan or grandiose ambition. They're boring companies that do the same thing over and over. They pay you a steady dividend and keep raising the amount of money you earn from them over time slowly and steadily. They don't have too many competitors. Even if they do, they're so huge that they don't have to worry too much about them. Their businesses have weathered many storms and have survived. They've seen it all and, as a result, handle most challenges before they even arise. As a result, there's nothing exciting going on with them, and the financial media doesn't pay them too much attention. All of this is very good news for you as an investor. Even better, when the markets fall, dividend-paying stocks (and the ETFs that track them) don't fall as much because of the guaranteed cash flow that these stocks produce. In fact, when the market does fall, dividend yields rise (thanks to prices falling), and it's a great opportunity for you to buy even more stock.

Diversification

This advantage pertains to index funds or ETF investing. With a single purchase, you'll manage to gain exposure to a wide variety of stocks, and your investments will be diversified automatically. Diversification is extremely important when it comes to passive investing. If you don't have time to analyze your investments too much, then you want to spread your risk as much as possible. Imagine you're invited to bet on a horse race but don't have much time to study the statistics horses' qualities. Instead, what you do is spread your money across the most likely horses to win and wait for results to come in.

A lot depends on the odds you're being offered, of course. However, by doing this, you're reducing your risk dramatically, and you're almost guaranteed to have a winning bet. The same principle applies to ETFs as well. The only difference is that you don't need to worry about the odds you're being offered. This makes it even easier for you to reduce your risk and achieve market average performance. Since your risk is spread out amongst so many stocks, the chances of your investment dropping to zero are nearly impossible. This is why targeting market average performance is far better than targeting market outperformance. When you try to achieve the highest returns in the market, you need to concentrate your investments in a single company or a handful of companies. In doing this, you're also exposing yourself to the risk of those companies failing. This is why so few people manage to outperform the markets.

Instruments

You've read about ETFs and index funds, so it's time to dive a bit deeper and understand how these instruments work. Truth be told, this isn't a complicated topic at all. There are just a few things to keep in mind before you invest in them.

Index Funds

Index funds are a type of mutual fund. A mutual fund, in turn, is an investment vehicle that allows everyday investors to gain exposure to a particular strategy. Mutual funds have managers who set the fund's strategy in place and then raise money as they execute it. For example, if you wish to gain exposure to smaller companies in the infrastructure sector in America, you can buy a mutual fund and gain exposure to their performance. The key thing to note about mutual funds is that they're usually designed to target market outperformance.

This targeting comes at a price. Investors pay fees to the tune of four to five percent every year, and this places a significant barrier to returns. Many mutual fund managers have reduced their fee rates to below two percent these days, but this is still a far cry from the 0.02% that the average index fund charges.

Over the last 100 years, most mutual funds have underperformed the market. This once again goes to show how market outperformance is immensely difficult to achieve. Instead, it's a lot better to target average market performance and keep contributing a steady sum towards it. Index funds were created to address the concern of high fees and poor performance. The pioneers in the field of index fund creation were the Vanguard Group. Funds offered by Vanguard continue to be the most popular investment choices in this field, and they continue to operate by charging extremely low fees. Mutual funds have some oddities in the way index funds behave. Every mutual fund has what is called a net asset value (NAV). This is the sum of its overall portfolio, divided by the number of units that have been issued. For example, a fund with $1 billion in assets (money to invest) that has issued one million units has a NAV of $1,000.

The NAV fluctuates according to the value of the stocks held in the mutual fund's portfolio. For example, if the market value of stocks in the portfolio adds up to $1,200, then this is the fund's new NAV. This number is determined at the end of each market day. Once the number is figured out, this is the price at which the mutual fund will trade the following day. This is irrespective of what happens to the individual stocks in the portfolio. Let's say the market value of the portfolio of stocks crashes to $900. You will still be able to buy and sell the mutual fund at $1,200. Index funds' prices, therefore, don't fluctuate during the market day. They're set once, and that's the price at which they trade throughout the next day.

ETFs

To address this disadvantage or oddity in mutual funds, ETFs were developed. ETFs have a NAV as well, but unlike mutual funds, their NAVs fluctuate throughout the day, much like the value of a common stock. This makes their prices fairer as the market day progresses. It's important to understand that ETFs, much like mutual funds, have a variety of strategies. You can find ETFs that charge a high amount of fees and chase returns through obscure strategies. You'll also find ETFs that follow the indexing strategy and generate returns in line with their indexes. These ETFs also have low fees like their index fund counterparts. One of the key advantages of an ETF over an index fund is that the ETF usually doesn't have any investment minimums. Typically, mutual funds impose minimums of $3,000 or more. However, you can buy a single unit of an ETF for whatever price it's selling.

Evaluation

Choosing a good index fund or ETF is crucial for achieving success with your passive income investment plan. The best way to do this is to read the prospectus that comes with the fund. The investment prospectus describes the strategy in detail and explains what kind of instruments the fund will be investing in.

When it comes to funds that track indexes, the prospectuses will be pretty short. As you've seen, the thesis behind indexing is pretty straightforward, and it doesn't need much fancy explanation. You can read this in a matter of a few minutes to understand what the strategy is. Pay attention to the index that the fund tracks. The criteria that the index is built on will be described in the prospectus, so read it to understand what you're buying into. For example, the Dividend Aristocrats index tracks companies that have raised their dividends for over 25 years. In contrast, the Dividend Achievers index tracks those that have raised their dividends for 10 years.

The primary difference between them is the latter targets capital gains growth as well. The Aristocrat stocks are already large companies, and you can't expect huge capital gains. The Achievers pay a certain dividend, but given that they're younger companies, they stand to earn more money as they grow and thus bring you capital gains. Pay attention to the index's issuer as well. Often fund issuers will create their own index to make lives easier for them. If they control the index's criteria, then they can change the rules as time goes by. Here are some of the high-quality fund issuers that you can invest in. All of these companies have been around for long are unlikely to engage in such shenanigans:

- Vanguard
- Fidelity
- T. Rowe Price
- Franklin Templeton
- iShares
- Nuveen Asset Management
- SPDR
- Charles Schwab

Some of these companies will have smaller funds that target different investment goals. You should stick to investing in the most passive of funds that charge low management fees and are at least $10 billion in size. When it comes to passive investing, there's strength in numbers, so make sure you evaluate these funds accordingly. Choose the ones with the lowest fees. Pay attention to how far the fund lags the index in terms of performance.

Funds cannot always match the index's performance accurately because the fund has expenses as well as trading fees to pay. As the weight of individual stocks in the index fluctuates, the fund manager needs to adjust their portfolio, and this creates fees. Look for the ones that have the smallest divergence. Keep in mind that the annual fees you pay are not included in this calculation. For example, you could have a fund that lags its index by 0.1% and charges 0.5% as fees versus another that lags by 0.2% but charges just 0.01% in fees. In such cases, the latter is a better investment because fees will eat into your gains over the long term, and it isn't worth paying for the higher performance.

Building a Portfolio

While your aim is to build a portfolio that passively brings in cash every year, your aim should be to construct a stable portfolio. This is because you want your passive income to be generated over a long period of time. If you chase the highest dividend yields, you'll likely be investing in something that isn't going to last very long.

You'll have to monitor it that much more and will have to repeatedly find new avenues of investment. Portfolio construction is a deeply debated topic, and it can be a bit confusing once you begin to dive deeply into it. Entire textbooks have been written on efficient portfolio construction, but I'm not going to bore you with all of these high finance topics. Instead, you should construct a portfolio that captures a piece of all the pies that are a part of the American economy. The first pie that you can capture is the performance of businesses in America.

Equity

Equity refers to an individual's ownership in a company or a business. As you've already learned, when you buy a share, you're buying ownership in a business. The first component of your portfolio should seek to capture the gains in ownership of American business. In other words, buy an ETF or an index fund that pays you dividends. You'll be indirectly investing in stocks and will gain whatever the performance these companies post. By insisting on dividends being paid, you'll create a margin of safety from the downside. I'll address the asset allocation question later in this section, but remember that equity should be a good chunk of your portfolio.

Fixed Income

Don't be misled by the term fixed income. The word implies constant payment of cash, but this is only the spirit of the asset class. In reality, fixed-income investments are just as risky as stocks. The primary instrument in the fixed income asset class is a bond. A bond is slightly different security from a stock. While stocks represent ownership, bonds represent credit. When you buy bonds from a company, you're lending them money equal to the amount you've paid for the bonds. In return, you'll earn an interest rate for a certain period of time. Here's where bonds can get confusing. Due to the fact that they can be traded freely in the markets between investors, the face value (amount of money you lend the company), and the price can be different. You can buy a $100 face value bond for $50. At the end of the bond term, you'll receive $100 back along with collecting whatever interest payments in the interim. Thus, it's possible to buy bonds with the intention of earning capital gains. This form of investment is just as risky and time-consuming as investing in common stocks is. Therefore, the best thing to do is to invest in an ETF that tracks bond indexes. You'll earn dividends in the form of interest payments.

The downside of fixed income investment is that their capital gains tend to be low. You can expect to earn around five percent every year. However, they hold their value a lot better since ETFs tend to invest in high-quality bonds. As a result, your cash flow is pretty much guaranteed. Of the five percent return, approximately 90% of it will be through dividends, with the rest being capital gains. Contrast this to the two to three percent yield stock dividends give you, and you can see how the higher cash flow can help fuel further investments. More importantly, fixed income moves in a largely opposite direction from equity. When stocks go down, investors typically rush to buy bonds, and this increases their prices. They form a good safety buffer against declining markets as a result.

Real Estate

Isn't real estate investing all about buying property? How can you invest in real estate through the stock market? Well, this is where real estate investment trusts come into the picture. REITs are companies that invest in real estate properties and earn money by collecting rents or selling those properties. They're mandated by law to payout 90% of their profits back to their investors. This means their dividend yields are a lot higher than regular common stock. REIT yields often average five to eight percent. However, like fixed income, their capital gains are lower due to the companies paying out such large amounts in cash.

From a passive investor's point of view, REITs are a great way to earn rental income. You can invest in ETFs that target certain types of real estate, or you can choose to invest in diversified ETFs. For example, you can buy an ETF that consists of hospital REITs or residential REITs. By doing this, you'll be gaining exposure to one particular type of real estate, and this can increase the risk in your portfolio. It's better to buy an ETF that targets broad, diversified REITs. In this way, you'll capture a piece of America's real estate market.

International Stocks

This asset class is a negative example. Don't bother investing in international stocks. You'll hear a lot about China's rise over the next decade, and everyone will be lining up to buy Chinese tech stocks or whatever else that country excels in. There's no denying that China's rise has created huge competition for the United States. However, when it comes to transparency and safeguarding shareholder rights, that country has a long way to go. Its entire system is designed around obscuring data, and as a result, any investment in China is extremely risky. This isn't the case with America, where you are assured of due process and transparent regulation.

It's fashionable to highlight how behind the times America has fallen, but the fact is that this country is still the best when it comes to safeguarding business interests and ownership rights. Your investment will not be seized by the government in the name of nationalization or "the people's good" or whatever it is governments can think of. The biggest disadvantage of international stock investment, even through an ETF, is that you're investing in a very different business culture.

This isn't limited to just China but to other economies such as the United Kingdom, the European Union, or Japan. Laws are different, and the factors that drive the economy are completely different. As a result, evaluating strengths and weaknesses is tricky. If you can devote time to study these economies, then, by all means, go ahead and invest. However, this is active investing and isn't passive. The objective of passive investing is to be able to forget about your investment and know that it's working away silently.

International stocks and companies don't have this quality in them, so stay away from them. Every once in a while, some foreign country starts getting mentioned in the news, and everyone jumps in and invests in them. In the 90s, it was the Asian tigers (Indonesia, Thailand, and another country that everyone has forgotten about). In the 2000s, India and Brazil were talked about as being rivals to China. India is dealing with an increasingly polarized citizenship, while Brazil is reeling from corruption. Both countries have quietly receded from the spotlight. China is the only country that has managed to raise itself from the lowest ranks and join the world's list of developed economies. Japan was spoken about as being a major potential competitor to America in the 80s and then promptly fell into a recession it has never recovered from. South Korea industrialized rapidly but lives in the shadow of a crackpot with his hand on a world-ending weapon.

Australia is a developed economy but is entirely dependent on Chinese buyers. As a result, it's completely dependent on whatever China does. The Scandinavian countries have high levels of development and free societies, but language barriers prevent a lot of their companies from becoming truly global presences. Besides, their populations are small (despite being wealthy), and as a result, companies can only grow so much. The Middle East needs no introduction when it comes to instability and crackpot rulers. It's a brave person who decides to invest in anything in that region. Even the most stable and developed place of that region, Dubai, witnesses property fluctuations of close to 10% every year on average. In short, don't try to outsmart yourself. Stay close to home and invest in things you can understand easily.

Allocation

So how much of your money should you allocate between equity, fixed income, and real estate? For starters, if you already have a mortgage or are earning rental cash flow from a property, you don't need to invest in REITs. You already have exposure to the market, and adding to it makes no sense. In this case, you can opt for a 70/30 split between equity and fixed income. The choice of which asset class receives the 70% allocation depends on your priorities. If you want to maximize cash flow, allocating 70% to fixed income makes sense. If you want a blend of cash flow and capital gain, a 70% allocation to equity works. Why not 50/50? Well, this is a no man's land allocation. Your portfolio will neither have large cash flow, nor will you be able to capture capital gains efficiently. To realize a strategy's benefits, you need to commit to it. This is why the majority of your capital should be allocated to a particular asset class. These are just guidelines, of course. You can increase it to 80/20 or 90/10. The more you increase allocations, the more committed you will be to an asset class. A 90/10 split isn't recommended. Stick to a minimum of 70% majority allocation and a maximum of 85%.

If you don't own real estate, then the REIT investment will come from your portfolio's fixed income portion. If you wish to maximize income, you can allocate 40% to REITs, 30% to fixed income, and 30% to equities that pay dividends. It's still a 70/30 split, but you've allocated 40% of the 70$ to REITs. REITs pay a higher amount of dividend income, and you can choose to invest in them entirely. However, it's wise to allocate some money to bonds since you don't want to be entirely dependent on real estate values. This is just intelligent diversification. Take these distributions out for a trial run for a year or so, and see how it works for you. If you're unhappy with it, you can tweak your allocations and redesign your portfolio. Remember to do all of this using ETFs. You'll need just three purchases at the most to design this portfolio.

There is a lot of information out there that ties portfolio allocation to risk. It can be confusing to think in these terms. Instead, ask yourself what your investment goal is and allocate your money accordingly. You'll earn cash flow, no matter what, when you pursue a dividend indexing strategy, so it's not as if you're losing out on anything. If you're someone who has time on their hands and is willing to invest it to create market outperformance, then the next chapter is for you.

Chapter 4:

Active Investing

Active market participation is a very different proposition from passive investing. There are two ways of making money in the markets. With passive investing, investors sit back and let the market do its thing. Their focus is the long term, and the best way to describe their approach would be to term it as a "set and forget" one. The active investor is not interested in the long term moves in the market. While passive investors adopt a timeline of at least a decade, passive investors rarely hold onto their positions (investments) for longer than a month. There are many strategies that active investors use to trade the markets over the short term.

You'll be learning some of these in this chapter. Before getting in them, it's important for you to understand the mindset behind short term investing or trading. This means you need to understand how the market works in the long term versus the short term. A company's stock price doesn't always reflect its true value. Value in this context refers to what its business is worth. The company produces cash flow by selling its products to its customers. This makes it an asset, and it's worth a certain amount of money. The company's stock is the easiest way to get a piece of this pie. However, the stock price fluctuates because there are many investors and traders who are looking to capture a piece of it as well. This leads to situations where the company's value and stock price diverge from one another. The stock price might be less than the intrinsic value, or it might be greater than it. A long term investor is concerned with buying the stock for a price that is equal to or less than its intrinsic value. This is because, over the long term, the stock's price will rise roughly in line with the earnings growth of the company. As long as the company performs well and conducts its business in accordance with good economic principles, you can expect its stock price to reflect this behavior. It might not be equal to intrinsic value at every stage of the rise, but there's no doubt that the growth rate will be the same, barring any unforeseen circumstances.

Take Apple, for instance. In 2001, the company had just launched the iPod, and Steve Jobs was on his way to becoming a Silicon Valley god. Apple's market value (as a company) was in the low billions at that point. Fast forward to today, and it's worth well over a trillion dollars. This is in line with the way the company has grown over the years and the various products it has released along with the international markets it has expanded into.

Amazon is another example of how a company's stock price has grown as the company has expanded. While you could argue that these companies' current valuations are not equal to their intrinsic value, there's no doubt that the rise in stock prices has reflected the rise in intrinsic value quite well.

Short term traders are not concerned with intrinsic value. They're concerned with the here and now. In the short term, prices change thanks to supply and demand. However, there's a bigger reason they move and diverge from intrinsic value. The reason is emotion. People express their emotions about a company through its stock price. Take Tesla, for instance. This company loses money on every car it manufactures and earns a profit thanks to government subsidies and energy credits (*Financials & Accounting | Tesla, Inc.*, 2019). Yet, the CEO of Tesla has been elevated to god-like status, and the market has turned him into a billionaire. Tesla is worth more than the bigger automakers combined, and this is used as proof to say that the company is the biggest and best car manufacturer in the world. Never mind the oddity of a car company making money thanks to government handouts and short term policies surrounding clean energy. Traders view such extreme emotion with great interest because it allows them to cash in on such moves. Tesla might rise in price thanks to increased demand. If the CEO announces something on his Twitter account, as he often does, then the price of the stock is likely to rise.

In short, traders look to take advantage of such emotional swings in the market. Emotion is not connected to the actual business, and this is why irrationality in the markets lasts for a while. For example, one of the biggest frauds in American corporate history was the energy trading giant Enron. The evidence of fraud was present for at least a year prior to its collapse (Mclean & Elkind, 2004):. However, the stock price rose nonetheless. Traders can become victims of such irrationality, but they can profit as well. Needless to say, profitable traders are the ones that take advantage of such situations.

There are many ways traders capture the emotional picture of the markets. Some use technical analysis while some use fundamental analysis involving macroeconomic factors. In this sense, short term or active investing provides more opportunities. In the long run, stock prices will either go up or down. In the short term, though, there's no end to the combination of moves that a stock can make. It could go up then fall down and then rise up again. It could go sideways and then rise and fall back down. Traders take advantage of these moves and trade in and out of the markets at a high rate. Let's look at some of the advantages of such an approach.

Advantages

There are many advantages to short term trading. I've already mentioned one of them. There is a greater combination of market moves for you to take advantage of. If you miss one short term move, another is likely to form soon. In this way, you're always in with a chance to make money.

Variety

Since short term investors are not concerned with the intrinsic value of their assets, it opens up the entire world of financial instruments to them. If you like how Bitcoin is moving right, you could trade it by jumping in and out quickly. You can trade bond interest rates or common stocks. You can trade derivatives of these bonds and stocks and not know a single thing about your trading asset. Obviously, you'll need to understand which economic factors move prices, but you don't need to understand the nitty-gritty of these assets, unlike with long term investing.

Active investing isn't a passive endeavor but you can turn it slightly passive by reframing your investment timelines. For example, you can trade options in a few instruments every month and then monitor your investments as time goes by. Options trades usually last for a month or so, and this means you need to put in some initial work and then focus on maintaining the trade. Alternatively, if this appeals to you, you could sit in front of the trading screen and religiously follow them. Some traders do this, and it suits their psyche. Some traders even designate certain months of the year during which they trade. For example, they trade the markets four or five months every year and do little else. They follow them on a minute by minute basis and don't focus on anything else. Once this period is over, they return to the real world and stay away from the markets. Trading allows you to do this since there's no end to the degree of customization you can create in your routine.

Many brokers offer a ton of options for the trader to customize their routines. You can trade the stock market, which gives you access to stocks, options, futures, bonds, and bond derivatives (if you have enough capital). I'll explain what these instruments are shortly. You can also trade commodities such as oil, gold, silver, platinum, etc. and make money through short-term cycles. Agricultural commodities such as corn and soybean are also traded heavily. If you have some insight into farming practices or weather patterns, you can earn money by trading these assets.

Opportunities

The short term trader simply has more opportunities than the long term investor. One of the reasons for this has been discussed already. Another reason is that the emotional factors surrounding prices change regularly. A good example of this was the behavior of oil recently. When the Covid-19 pandemic first hit and lockdowns started occurring, oil suppliers found that there was no one buying their oil. China is one of the biggest consumers of oil, and thanks to them locking down their economy, oil was simply lying around without any demand. Combine this with the panic that was setting in thanks to uncertainty and world-ending prophecies, the price of oil sank to negative territory. The real price of oil was not negative, but it was extremely low thanks to the nonexistent demand. However, this was a short term correction. It wasn't as if the world would not need oil all of a sudden. The commodity had been trading in the 20s before the pandemic hit, and at the very least, prices would rise back to that level once things normalized. Intelligent traders could have bought oil futures for low prices and then held onto their position as demand steadily rose back up. Oil is now trading in the low 40s, which indicates the size of the opportunity that was present.

Similarly, gold and silver presented massive opportunities, as well. These precious metals are often seen as a safe haven when the value of paper money declines. With every crisis, governments around the world print more money and effectively borrow money from the future. This means inflation (remember this?) rises, and the value of money decreases. Gold and silver are historic means of monetary exchange, and thus, their prices will increase. Gold is currently trading at record highs, breaking the $2,000 per ounce barrier. Silver has risen even more dramatically, and while it isn't at record highs, silver investors have undoubtedly been very happy with their holdings.

Such opportunities are not always available to the long term passive investor. The active investor's mindset allows them to take more risk with their investments. Passive investors look to minimize activity as much as possible, resulting in them missing some opportunities. I should make it clear that this isn't about which type of investing is "better." The best form of investment is something that suits your mindset. Some people handle the rigors of active investment a lot better than others. Some prefer to automate their investments and do nothing. Each method works, and you need to match your preferences to them.

Freedom

Passive investing takes time. Most of the gains you will create will remain unrealized for a long time—active investing results in gains in shorter time frames. Suppose you happen to have enough ideas to take advantage of the markets, either through technical analysis methods or through the analysis of macroeconomic factors. In that case, you'll end up creating an asset that has a steady cash flow. A lot depends on how well you can execute your strategies, of course. It isn't as if active investing is guaranteed to bring you a large number of profits. However, the steady flow of gains gives you the ability to exponentially grow your wealth. Consider the following example.

If you passively invest $1,000 and continue to invest this amount over the course of 20 years, you'll have $64,000 in the bank (assuming a 10% growth rate.) If you manage to invest $1,000 into a short term trading opportunity and manage to earn 10% on it, your rate of return is far higher than the 10% yearly number that passive investing gives you. If you keep earning this return every month or so, you could double your money in no time. This, in turn, creates more freedom in your lifestyle, and you'll be able to enjoy your money more. I must warn you that it's easy to blur the line between this mode of thinking and 'get rich quick' style thinking. Many people are drawn to trading because they want to get rich quickly. This is what makes trading so difficult. It doesn't have anything to do with how tough it is. It's just that most people's mindsets are not suited for trading.

Instruments

As I mentioned earlier, there is a wide variety of instruments available for you to trade. You need to understand how all of them work to take advantage of their short term moves.

Stocks

You've already learned all about stocks and how they work. You can trade stocks of companies in the short term. However, most traders don't do this unless they have less than $1,000 in capital. This is because stock trades take some time to settle. Typically, they take two business days. If you sell stock on Monday, you won't receive your cash back until Wednesday. This makes entering the market quickly a bit difficult. However, it is possible to speculate in stocks successfully. If you happen to be a more laid back trader, then trading these might be perfect for you.

Bonds

Like stocks, you've already learned about bonds. The best speculative bonds happen to be junk bonds. These pay a very high interest rate due to the lack of investment safety in them. Even good companies issue junk bonds once in a while because they're unsecured. Unlike high-quality bonds, junk bonds are not collateralized by company assets. Therefore, if the company defaults on their payment, the bondholder receives nothing but a slip of paper saying they're out of luck. However, every once in a while, a bond that is secured and has a low chance of default is issued. This results in the investor earning a high interest rate, usually over 10%, and the price of the bond rising as the rest of the market realizes that this junk bond isn't going to default.

Bond prices are always quoted in percentage terms. For example, if a bond is selling for $10,000 and if its face value is $50,000, it's price is quoted as 20. This is because 10,000 is 20% of 50,000. Junk bonds typically never sell for their face value and start off selling for 50 or less. If the bond doesn't default, then the investor can buy it at 50 and receive the full face value back upon maturity. Thus, not only do they earn a steady 10% or greater interest, but they also realize a capital gain of 50% upon maturity. If maturity occurs in 2 years, that's a gain of 25% per year before taking interest into account. Not a bad play! Having said that, there's a reason these bonds are labeled "junk." The investor needs to carefully consider the merits of investing in such bonds and must evaluate the company's financial statements to make sure the risk of default is lower than usual.

Futures

Futures contracts are derivative instruments. A derivative is a financial instrument that derives its value from something else. Futures are contracts that promise the sale of an underlying asset at a certain price on a certain date. For example, oil futures that expire in a month's time and are selling for $45 state that the buyer of the contract will receive X number of barrels of oil for $45 in a month's time. The variable "X" depends on the individual contract. For example, oil contracts usually cover 1,000 barrels of oil. Gold futures cover 1 oz. of the metal, as do silver contracts. Soybean and corn futures cover 5,000 bushels of the commodity. Futures are typically used by firms that depend on the commodities as a part of their business. For example, airlines often buy a large quantity of jet fuel futures to predict the cost of fuel they'll incur. Oil trading firms buy oil futures when the commodity is being transported from one port to another.

If the price of oil were to fluctuate massively during transit, they'd be exposed to large losses. The futures contract ensures they won't have to worry about what prices will be once their oil is delivered.

I must mention that most futures contracts don't guarantee the delivery of the underlying product. The way it works is that designated firms are eligible to receive delivery of the product, but the average trader or investor is not. After all, it's hard to think of what you could do with a 1,000 barrels of oil delivered to your doorstep. Futures, therefore, end up being mostly financial instruments to speculate in. You can buy and sell them or even do what's called a rollover. If you're holding a contract that expires at the end of this month, you can roll your position over so that it expires the next month. If you don't sell your contract or cover your position by the expiry date, your broker will automatically do this for you.

Futures exist on stocks, commodities, and bonds. Bond derivatives are usually available to those who have over $10 million in capital. Some brokers also issue futures contracts on forex rates, but these are rare. The biggest advantage that futures offer is the ability to leverage your investment. When you buy shares of stock, you need to pay the entire amount upfront. If you buy 100 shares at $10 each, you'll have to pay $1,000. If you buy a single futures contract that covers 100 shares, you don't need to pay $1,000. You might have to pay $200 or even $100. This is because every futures contract allows you to trade on what is called margin. Margin refers to the equity you have in your account. Equity is the sum of cash and other trading positions' value in your account. Every futures contract specifies the margin required to trade it. Some contracts have 10% margins, while others have 50%. It depends on the underlying instrument. By depositing a smaller amount with your broker, your cash on cash return is a lot higher, and this boosts your account's growth.

Let's say you paid $200 to control $1,000 worth of instruments. If the value of the overall position increases from $1,000 to $1,200 (a 20% gain), your cash on cash return is 100% ($200 return on $200 cash invested.) This situation is referred to as leverage in financial circles. Leverage boosts your returns, but it can also bankrupt you. If the price of the asset drops by 20%, you'll lose your entire investment. Even worse, if it drops by 50%, you'll now owe an amount greater than your original investment. There are ways to manage leverage and risk in your investments, so it isn't as if this is a deal-breaker. However, you need to be very careful when employing leverage and not use too much of it in an attempt to earn outsized gains.

Options

Options are a very popular instrument when it comes to speculation. These are also derivatives, like futures, but they behave a bit differently. An options contract gives you the right to buy or sell the underlying asset for a certain price before a certain date. The price at which you can buy or sell the underlying asset is called the strike price. The date before which you can do this is called the expiry date.

There are two kinds of options contracts that will be available to you when you begin trading. These are calls and puts. A call allows you to buy the underlying while the put allows you to sell it. Investors buy calls if they believe that prices will rise. For example, if the underlying stock is selling for $50 and if they believe it'll rise to $100, they buy calls on the stock at $70. Once the stock rises past $70, they exercise the option and sell it at the market price (which is greater than $70) and earn a profit. Similarly, buyers of puts make money when prices of the underlying fall. The underlying instrument on which options are created are typically stocks or forex instruments. Forex options are also rare, so really, all you'll see is stock options. Options trading is a deeply complex topic, and many strategies exist in this space. There are a number of books on this topic that do it justice.

Let's say you've noticed a stock whose price has been in a narrow range. There's an important piece of news that is coming up, and you're not sure whether this news will be good or bad. All you know is that whatever the news is, the stock price is going to explode either up or down. If you were trading the stock itself, this puts you in an unsafe position. What if you buy the stock, but the news turns out to be bad, and the stock plummets? If only there was a way for you to profit no matter what direction the stock moves in. This is what options allow you to do. This strategy is called the straddle trade. You buy a call that is a few levels up from the current market price. This ensures if prices explode upwards, you'll be in a profit. You then buy a put that is a few levels below current market prices. Thus, if prices fall, you'll profit as well.

When you buy an option, irrespective of whether it's a call or a put, you pay what is called a premium. The premium is the cost of the options contract, and it is non-refundable. You need to subtract the option premium from the overall profit of your trade. If the stock price mentioned just now rises, the value of the put would decline to zero. However, the call premium will increase in line with the rise in prices. Thus, your overall profit in the trade will equal the price rise minus the options premiums you paid on trade entry. The net result is that you have a nondirectional bet in the market, and you don't care which way prices move. All you care about is the degree of the movement. A similar trade to the straddle is the strangle which is used for even more explosive situations. Each options contract covers 100 shares of the underlying stock. Therefore, you need to multiply the price of the option by 100 to figure out how much you need to pay. Options are perhaps the best bet for you to speculate in since they allow you to dramatically lower your risk in the markets and allow you to profit no matter which way stock prices move.

Forex

Forex isn't an instrument as much as it is another market entirely. The forex market is, in fact, the biggest market in the world, amounting to $10 trillion in size. This dwarfs the stock markets of the world by many multiples. Forex is a very unique market and has a different set of rules.

The first condition is that the market never closes. Given that the instruments being traded in it are global currencies, the market never closes since it's always 9 A.M. somewhere in the world. The forex market day is divided into three sessions. The first session begins in Auckland, New Zealand, and is called the Asian session. It gathers pace as Sydney, Tokyo, Hong Kong, and Singapore come online. As the day moves on, Europe starts waking up. Geneva, Frankfurt, Paris, and then London come fully online and this is the European session. The Asian and European sessions overlap for a couple of hours.

As the European session wears on, and as Asia is firmly asleep, North America comes online. The final four hours of Europe (London), and the first few hours of New York overlap and this is the most heavily traded portion of the day. Eventually, London closes, and New York moves on. After New York closes at 5 P.M. eastern, Dallas and San Francisco take over to a small extent. This is a dead period, though, since no major financial center is online. At midnight eastern, Auckland wakes back up, and volumes begin increasing. The market closes only on Saturday and Sunday. However, given the time overlaps, Sunday isn't a complete rest day since Asia opens late on Sunday eastern time.

The instruments are also unique. Forex instruments are currency pairs. For example, the most popular currency pair is the EURUSD, which is the Euro and the U.S Dollar. Pairs exist for nearly every currency in the world. This allows you to speculate on the economic direction of a particular country. Keep in mind that not every country allows its currency to fluctuate freely in the markets. China is a known currency manipulator and tightly controls the flow of its currency. However, there are many currency pairs you can speculate in, so it isn't as if you need the Renminbi to profit. Forex trading is as deep a topic as options trading is, so you should refer to other books on this topic. Most forex traders use a combination of technical analysis and macroeconomic analysis to profit. Technical analysis refers to the use of indicators and other tools that are developed by calculating price movements. The biggest advantage of forex is that you can choose your hours of operation. Unlike the stock market that is open for a few hours every day, forex markets are always open, and thus, you can trade whenever you like. This is helpful if you work at a full-time job.

ETFs

You can use ETFs to speculate on the short term direction of the markets as well as invest for the long term passively. ETFs, as you know, have a wide variety of investment objectives. Some ETFs track indexes and are passive instruments. Others are highly speculative and offer the chance of earning outsized gains. These ETFs are usually leveraged and appended with terms such as "2X" or "3X." The number refers to the degree to which the ETF will move, given a change in its underlying portfolio. For example, there are ETFs that are leveraged on the S&P 500. If the index moves up by a single point, these ETFs will move twice or thrice that amount. Of course, if the index moves down by a point, the ETF will decrease in price by a greater amount.

The fund manager achieves this result by maintaining a constant leverage ratio. In terms of long term investment, such ETFs are not safe. High levels of leverage are unsustainable over the long run, and at some point, adverse market conditions will put these funds in trouble. However, if your aim is to benefit from short term price moves, then such ETFs make a lot of sense. There are other ETFs that move in the opposite direction from their underlying index. These are called inverse ETFs. If you think the S&P 500 is about to go down, buying an inverse ETF will allow you to profit without having to short any instrument.

Shorting is the process of selling an instrument before buying it. In this method, your broker borrows shares for you to sell, and once prices decline, you cover the position by buying the shares back. Shorting sounds complicated, but from a trader's perspective, it's pretty straightforward. The problem is that you'll be borrowing stocks to short, and this means paying interest and maintaining a certain level of equity in your account. If you cannot maintain these margin levels, your broker will close the position and recover all funds from you. This situation is made worse when the market moves against you.

Inverse ETFs are essentially short-selling the underlying index. However, you simply buy the ETF, so there's no need for you to go on margin. The issue once again is that you cannot be invested for the long term. Technically you can, but it's a risky proposition. The mother of all speculative ETFs are leveraged inverse ETFs. These move in the opposite direction to the underlying index and move in multiples of those movements. You'll often see them labeled as being inverse 2X or 3X ETFs. These are highly speculative, and you should be on your toes when buying these. However, if you use them intelligently, you can make a lot of money in a short time. Best of all, you don't need to worry about borrowing money or stock. Simply buy them and sit back as they increase in value.

Keys to Success

There are many ways in which you can implement short term trading strategies. You can follow the market in five-minute intervals and exit your positions within a few hours. Or you could speculate in options and hold onto a position for a month or more. Whatever your strategy is, there are a few key principles to keep in mind.

Understand Your Strategy

This is a big issue with many traders who fail. They simply don't take the time to fully understand their strategy. They project gains by viewing prior market action and think that they'll achieve success easily. However, the live market environment is a different beast, and soon, they find that making money is not easy at all. This results in them losing money, and soon, their mental state gets affected. This results in a downward spiral as their results get worse. Such traders are also guilty of jumping from one strategy to the next in search of their holy grail. The fact is that such things don't exist in the markets.

No strategy is better than another. At the end of the day, you need to execute what works for you. As long as you do this, no one cares how you make money. Some people trade the markets after reading astrological signs. It isn't just individuals doing this but hedge funds! As long as they make money, who cares what their strategy is? Simple strategies make as much money as complicated ones. It all comes down to how well you understand and can execute your plans.

Manage Risk

This is the second pillar of trading. Along with understanding your strategy thoroughly, you need to figure out how much you're risking in your trades. Risk a small percentage of your account on every trade, preferably less than two percent. This means even if leverage moves against you, you're unlikely to lose a lot of money and will have enough in the bank to guard against these moves. Risk management often comes down to discipline. Fix a routine that works for you and stick to it no matter what. Monitor yourself psychologically. Remember that traders are concerned with predicting short term price movements. To do this successfully, you need to have a good handle on your own mindset. If you're all over the place, you can hardly expect to be able to predict the moves of other traders.

Use Money You Can Lose

Many people jump into trading with all of their life savings. This is an extremely irrational move. You should only speculate with money that you can fully afford to lose. Ensure you have enough savings in your bank account and have a solid passive investment portfolio. Once these are in place, set aside a small amount every month to speculate with. This way, you're not going to be emotionally invested in the outcomes of your trades, and you'll be able to maintain an even keel. Emotions will not take you out of profitable positions, and you won't buy or sell at the worst possible moment. Many traders set themselves up for failure by doing the opposite of this. This is indicative of a get rich quick mindset. It does not work that way. Instead, aim to execute your processes well, and everything will take care of itself. The stock market offers a number of ways for you to profit and create passive income. However, one of the best ways of earning passive income has nothing to do with the stock market at all.

Chapter 5:

The Best Passive Income Model

When it comes to passive income generation and wealth building in general, not many things come close to real estate. There are so many different ways of earning money with real estate that it's pretty much a no-brainer for anyone to get into if their objective is to make money. The thing to note with real estate is that the strategies require you to conduct a lot of work upfront and then maintain your asset periodically. Thus, it isn't completely passive in terms of activity. However, the cash on cash return and the ability to safely leverage your investment means it's a great way for beginners to invest. Beginners to real estate often shy away from the field thanks to the lingo. This is especially true of younger investors who feel the financial system might shut them out of the space. While credit criteria do ensure that the barrier of entry is lower for older individuals, this doesn't mean younger people cannot participate.

In this chapter, you're going to learn all about the various modes of real estate investment. You've already learned about REITs and how they work. If none of these methods work for you, you can get started with REIT investing to build your real estate portfolio.

The first thing to understand about real estate investing is that it's going to cost you money. Nowhere is the adage "It takes money to make money" truer than with real estate. Having said that, the amount of cash it takes is not exorbitant. With good planning, you can begin purchasing property relatively early. The key to making this work is to plan ahead of time. A large part of a real estate investment deal is the financing. Central to the financing portion of the deal is the mortgage. Understanding how they work and the things lenders look for in an application is the key to getting started.

Mortgages and Financing

Before getting into mortgages, you might be wondering if it's worth it to buy a property in full (called buying in cash)? This is possible. Most people don't do this because they like to use leverage to boost their returns safely. Also, most people don't have six figures of cash lying around to invest. Financing, therefore, is a necessity in almost every real estate transaction. Smart investors who have money to invest fully use leverage since it boosts their returns. There are different types of lenders you can approach for a loan. The most common lender is your local bank.

The bank's job is to loan people money and earn profits off the interest on the loan. Naturally, given that they're lending a lot of cash, banks do a thorough job of vetting their applicants. Experienced investors and those known to the bank qualify easily. However, this doesn't mean new applicants are turned away.

Before pursuing your first real estate deal, it's helpful to apply for pre-qualification with the bank. Pre-qualification is a process where the bank will let you know how much they can lend you and at what interest rates. It doesn't guarantee financing approval, but it does take you 90% of the way. At the end of the process, you'll receive a letter from the bank stating the terms of your mortgage, tentatively. You can use this letter to prove to sellers that you're a serious buyer. In some markets, sellers insist on pre-qualification since they're inundated with offers from less than capable buyers. So what does the mortgage approval process look like?

Numbers

The mortgage application process involves a lot of paperwork. Most people find this tedious because they don't prepare in advance and rush about trying to source relevant paperwork. Prepare in advance, and this will go by smoothly. Here are the most important documents you need to have ready:

- Proof of employment - A letter as well as pay stubs
- Tax returns over the past three years
- Proof of debt payments
- Bank statements for the past six months at the very least
- Brokerage, or other investment account statements
- If self-employed
    - Business licenses
    - Business bank statement for the past three years
    - Audited financial statements showing increasing or stable net income
    - Tax returns for the past three years
- Any other statement that shows ownership of an asset

The lender collects all of this information along with one other important number: Your FICO (Fair Isaac Corporation) score. This is also referred to as your credit score. Before you start gathering all of your information and documents, you can research your credit score through a number of ways.

If you have a credit card, the bank will almost certainly have a scheme where you can access your credit report for free once every year. Note that a credit report will often not contain your credit score. Check with your bank if this is the case. If they don't disclose your credit score, you can apply for this from one of the three major credit reporting agencies: Experian, Equifax, and TransUnion. Alternatively, you can apply to FICO itself. Some banks will offer you a VantageScore. This is pretty much the same thing as the FICO score, so it works as well. If your score is less than 680, you're going to have a hard time qualifying for a mortgage from a traditional lender. You're better off choosing some of the alternatives mentioned later in this chapter. Note that the application process is pretty much the same, so don't skip this section. Assuming your credit score is greater than 680, the lending officer starts compiling their report. Two figures are key to this report: the front ratio and back ratio. The front ratio is a measure of how well you can bear the expected mortgage expense. The back ratio compares all of your debt to your total income every month.

The front ratio is calculated by dividing your mortgage payment by your total income. Lenders look for this number to be less than 28%. If your monthly income is $2,000 and if your prospective mortgage payment is greater than $560, you're probably not going to qualify. Next is the back ratio. This is calculated by dividing your total debt burden by your monthly income. If you have car payments of $200 credit card debt payments of $100 per month and student loan debt payments worth $300 per month, your total debt burden is (100+200+300+mortgage payment). This ratio should be less than 33%. Some lenders stretch this to 36%, but this is a rare case. There's an additional wrinkle to these ratios. In extenuating circumstances, lenders disregard these ratios. If you have a large pile of cash saved up or if your brokerage statement shows substantial investments, lenders might be willing to let a high ratio slide. It's up to the individual loan officer, really. Once everything is calculated, the lender will offer you a certain interest rate and will specify the terms of financing.

Terms

Typically, lenders will expect you to pay some money upfront. This is called the down payment, and a traditional lender will expect you to pay at least 20% of the property value down. If the property is worth $100,000, you'll have to pay $20,000. Some of the other options have lower down payment requirements, so don't be intimidated by this just yet. Aside from the down payment, you'll have to pay closing costs. The typical real estate transaction involves a lot of professionals such as real estate agents, title deed agents, title insurance firms, and so on. These people need to get paid, and this is done via closing costs. Closing costs are usually between two to five percent of a deal. On a $100,000 property, you'll need to pay a maximum amount of $5,000. Many people ignore closing costs and focus only on their down payment. This leaves them scrambling for cash when the time comes. Don't be one of these people. Your interest rate plays a large role in the deal since this is what determines your monthly payment every month. Your monthly payment contains an interest portion and a principal portion. Every month you'll, therefore, be repaying interest as well as reducing your principal.

When buying property, it's best to pay as much as possible down. This reduces your monthly payment. It's also important for you to generate cash flow from your property. This is what ensures you'll be creating an asset and not a liability. If you assume a mortgage and then live in the home yourself without cash flow, you've just created a liability for yourself. I'll address the question of how to generate cash flow later in this chapter. For now, let's move on and look at some alternative financing options.

FHA

FHA stands for Federal Housing Authority, and it's the arm of the government that is tasked with providing loans for people. The great thing about the FHA is that it's backed by the U.S Government and therefore, can adopt a less strict framework when it comes to qualification. While traditional lenders require applicants to possess a credit score greater than 680, the FHA's minimum credit score requirement is 500 (*FHA Loan Refinance and Home Purchase Loans at FHA.Com*, 2020). What's more, if your credit score is greater than 580, you'll only need to pay three percent down. You'll just have to pay $3,000 instead of $20,000 down if you opt for the FHA.

If your credit score is below 580, you'll have to pay 10% down, which is still a lot less than a traditional lender's requirement. The loan application process is the same as with a traditional lender. You don't have to apply to a government office. Instead, the FHA works with a number of traditional lenders to provide loans. Ask your local bank if they're FHA approved or ask a realtor for this information. There are a few things you need to remember when using an FHA loan. Some people might find that a traditional loan makes more sense. Due to the low down payment requirement, you'll have to pay mortgage insurance, called PMI, every month. These costs can add up over the lifetime of the mortgage. You might have to pay more upfront with a traditional lender, but your monthly payment might be less, thanks to the absence of PMI.

Traditional lenders charge PMI if your down payment is less than 20%, but this is waived when you reach 20% equity in your home (you've paid 20% of the total home's value). However, FHA loans don't waive this, so make sure you calculate how much extra you're paying over the course of the mortgage. The other condition that FHA loans impose is the applicant has to use the property as their primary residence. Due to this, you cannot finance a property that you plan on renting out to someone else. Unless you live on the property, you cannot qualify for an FHA loan.

Lastly, the FHA does not approve of home flippers for some reason. Due to this, you cannot buy a property that has been sold within the past three months. Let's say person A buys a rundown property and rehabs it and places it back for sale within three months of first buying the property. You cannot buy this home from person A since it's against FHA criteria. Despite all of this, you can use FHA loans to generate cash flow every month. You'll learn how in the next section.

Hard Money

Some real estate strategies, such as home flipping, do not attract financing from traditional or FHA lenders. As a result, most entrepreneurs who wish to implement these strategies approach hard money lenders. These are private lending institutions, and their rates and criteria are not as attractive as traditional lenders' are. For starters, a hard money lender will require you to pay at least 30% down on the property. In some states, it's as high as 45%. When it comes to rehab, the lender will want you to pay this percentage on the adjusted recovery value (ARV) of the property. This is what the property will be worth once it's repaired.

The interest rates these lenders charge are also higher than what traditional lenders charge. As a result, most home flippers and rehabbers use hard money as what is called a bridge loan. Since traditional banks will not touch a rehab property, the real estate investor uses hard money to finance the deal in the first year.

Once the property is fully rehabbed and is occupied by tenants, they approach a traditional lender. With the risk now gone, the bank finances the property, and pays the hard money lender. In short, hard money bridges the gap between the rundown state of the property to the fully repaired condition, hence the name of the loan. Aside from hard money, you can even approach private investors and offer them a percentage of profits from the deal. Friends and family are also sources of funding you can tap in to. In a typical real estate deal, the order of steps to be executed is as follows:

- Determine your strategy
- Get pre-approval
- Locate a property
- Get financing and close the deal
- Execute your strategy

In some cases, you won't need to get pre-approval. The point of walking you through financing upfront was to show you that it isn't as complicated as it sounds. It's the lengthiest part of the process, so it pays to be prepared beforehand.

Investment Strategies

There are a number of real estate investment strategies you can implement. In this section, I'm going to walk you through all of them. These strategies work really well for residential real estate properties and for some commercial properties. Most real estate investors opt to invest in residential real estate since it's easy to obtain financing, and there's always a steady demand for it. Commercial real estate doesn't have different rules. It's just that banks view them differently, and the financing terms you'll receive aren't as favorable. Banks place a huge deal of importance on your experience in the field and on how well you can operate the property. You'll be leasing it to a store or some commercial venture, so it's important to take their business into account as well when calculating your cash flow. If this is your first time investing in real estate, stick to residential properties. Let's begin with the first strategy you can utilize.

Wholesaling

If you lack the resources to get started with your own property, then real estate wholesaling might be great for you. I must mention that wholesaling real estate is a grey area, but it's possible to do so legally. Just make sure you aren't stuck being a wholesaler for the entirety of your career!

A wholesaler puts a seller and a buyer into contact with one another. If this sounds familiar, it's what a real estate agent does. The agent receives a commission from the seller for doing this. A wholesaler does not necessarily have a real estate license. This is frowned upon in the real estate community. However, there is a demand for such people because wholesalers often locate properties that fly under the radar of major investors and realtors in the area. A property that requires significant upgrades, for instance, will not interest any realtor. There's no way they could convince a buyer to take this property. Given the depressed price, their commissions will also be low.

Real estate agents aim to sell the most expensive properties in the area since they are easy to market. It earns them huge commissions. As a wholesaler, this gives you a gap in the market. The key to wholesaling is to be able to work on identifying properties for sale as well as buyers with enough cash to buy the property. It's a tricky balance to get right. Most sellers will not talk to you unless you show them you have enough money to buy their property. Most buyers will not talk to you unless there are deals you can show them that make sense for them. Buyers have all kinds of strategies, so keeping their preferences in mind is important. It makes no sense to try and sell a rehab property to a turnkey rental investor. You'll learn what this is shortly. The best way to attract both buyers and sellers is to place signs at major traffic intersections. Have you ever driven around and seen those "We buy ugly houses!" signs? That's a wholesaler in action.

A good place to find sellers is by simply driving around the neighborhood and looking at properties that seem run down or out of shape. Post a flyer in their mailbox telling them you can find them a buyer. Another option is to send direct mail postcards to homeowners. You can find their addresses in the local county records office. Buyers can be found at local real estate investment club meetups. Every locality has one, and you'll be able to network with people here. Once you do establish a relationship with a buyer, let them know you'll bring them deals and that they should have proof of finances ready. This can be a letter from their bank or a copy of their six months' bank statement. Approach a seller with this information, but obscure the name of your investor and their contact information. This will prevent the seller from going behind your back. Negotiate a price that makes sense for all parties. Here's how the deal works. The seller signs a purchase agreement with you. You then assign the deal for a higher price to your buyer.

Let's say you find a property worth $50,000. You assign the sales agreement to your buyer for $60,000. You thus earn a $10,000 profit. When you sign the agreement with the seller, the agent involved in the deal will set up an escrow account. There will also be an escrow account between you and the buyer. Once the buyer transfers funds to the second escrow account, you withdraw the cash and keep your profit. You then transfer the remaining amount to the first escrow account. Thus, you earn your profit, and no one gets to know one another until the deal is finished.

The key thing to look for is the ability to assign the contract. This is as easy as looking at the signature page and looking for the word "assigns". That gives you the right to transfer the contract to someone else. An attorney can prepare this. You should also be upfront with the seller that the end buyer is someone else and that they'll need to be willing to assign the contract. This is a hit or miss strategy since some sellers will object to you making money on the deal. Some buyers might object to you making too much cash as well. Buyers who work with wholesalers are experienced, and they're up to speed with market rates. They're unlikely to allow you to earn more than $10,000 on a deal. However, when you consider that your investment is zero, even a couple deals will bring you enough money for a downpayment. Use this capital to execute the other strategies below.

House Hacking

House hacking should be the default investment approach that first time home buyers ought to take, barring special circumstances. The term has been coined in the past decade and makes it seem as if it's an extremely complicated strategy. However, this is just marketing. House hacking has been around for ages now, and smart investors who recognize how money works have always used it. The premise is simple. Your objective is to earn as much rent as possible so that your mortgage payment is either reduced significantly or even eliminated. This strategy works very well for people who live close to college towns. You'd think otherwise, but real estate around colleges tends to be highly priced. This is due to the steady demand from university students. This means rental prices are high and you can partition homes to house a larger number of people than you would in a suburb. This means there is a good chance that the rental income will pay the mortgage every month. In some areas, it might even leave you with excess cash. However, let's take a step back and examine the first step you need to take.

The first thing to do is to locate a good property. Multi-family properties are best for this. These are properties that have separate units within them. The traditional off-campus student house containing five rooms or more also works, although this is an example of a single-family property. House hacking assumes that you will be living in the property. In the case of a single-family home, you'll be occupying one of the rooms and renting the remaining rooms out. In a multi-family property, you'll be occupying one of the units and renting the rest of them out. The reason house hacking is so powerful is because you can use an FHA loan to reduce your down payment to just three percent. This reduces your cash investment dramatically. As long as the rent pays the mortgage, you'll keep building equity in the property and will eventually get paid to own it.

There are a few key steps to take when working the math of the property. The first is to look at the property's monthly rental income as a percentage of the property value. A good property to house hack will earn at least one percent of the property's value in rent every month. If the property is worth $100,000, it must produce at least $1,000 in rental income. This is called the one percent rule and solves a lot of issues for you. You'll have to maintain the property, so you can assume that half of this will be eaten up by costs. Therefore, your cash flow from the property in question will amount to $500 per month. I must point out: when calculating rental income for the one percent rule, you need to include your own unit's rent as well. In real life, you'll be living there and won't pay rent but, calculate the numbers as if you were. From the example above, if you occupy one unit, the total rent might decrease to $800. This will leave you with roughly $400 per month. Let's say you receive a 3.07% interest rate from the FHA. Here's what the numbers look like on your loan:

- Down payment = $3,000
- Closing costs = $3,000
- Mortgage interest rate = 3.07%
- Term = 30 years
- Monthly mortgage payment = $544
- Monthly rental income = $800
- Rental income after costs = $400
- Net cash outflow = Mortgage payment - Rental income after costs = 544 - 400 = $144
- Total cash invested = Down payment + Closing costs = $6,000

In this deal, you've invested $6,000 upfront for a three percent stake in a property that you're paying $144 per month over the course of 30 years to own. That's a great deal! You'll have paid a total of (144*12*30 + 6000) $57,840 out of pocket to own a $100,000 property. If you weren't earning the rental income, you would have paid (544*12*30 + 6000) = $201,840 for the same property. That's a reduction of 71% in costs! Here's how you can make this a better deal, though. What if you paid 40% down?

- Down payment = $40,000
- Closing costs = $3,000
- Mortgage interest rate = 3.07%
- Term = 30 years
- Monthly mortgage payment = $387
- Monthly rental income = $800

- Rental income after costs = $400
- Net cash inflow = Mortgage payment - Rental income after costs = 400 - 387 = $13
- Total cash invested = Down payment + Closing costs = $43,000

In this scenario, you're investing $43,000 upfront and getting paid $13 every month to live in the property and own it. The higher your down payment is, the lower your monthly mortgage will be. This assumes a 30-year term. You could pay $466 out of pocket and own this in 20 years as well. At some point, you might want to move to another home. This is when you can refinance this property using a traditional mortgage. Then, your monthly rental income after expenses rises to $500. Assuming your terms remain the same, you'll get paid to own this property in 20 years. You can use the mortgage payment calculator at **https://www.bankrate.com/calculators/mortgages/mortgage-calculator.aspx** to figure out these numbers.

You can locate great house hacking deals using your local realtor. A key component of a successful house hack is becoming a landlord. You'll need to attract high-quality tenants and invest in your property to make sure it's up to the standards they expect. Good tenants stay for longer, and you won't have payment collection issues with them. You also want to make sure you can afford the monthly mortgage payment. You never know what might happen. If your property lies vacant for over a year, you'll need to pay the mortgage out of pocket. This is why estimating costs at 50% of rental income works well. These costs won't be incurred in this proportion every month, but it's best to set aside this amount as cash in the bank. There isn't much else to house hacking. Make sure you run the numbers thoroughly and only purchase deals where they make sense. This is why pre-approval is crucial since it will tell you roughly what you can expect your mortgage payment will be.

Turnkey Rentals

This mode of investment is similar to a house hack, except you won't be living in the property. It can also be turned into a pretty passive investment. Turnkey rentals refer to properties that are ready to be rented. Often, they'll have people living in them already and will be producing cash flow for you. These properties usually sell above the average prices for the area they're located in. After all, they won't need much work other than a lick of paint every now and then. The presence of tenants is also an extremely attractive option for potential investors. Locating them is easy thanks to websites such as Zillow and Roofstock.

Local realtors will know these properties well since they'll stand to earn high commissions from selling them. The one percent rule is extremely important when it comes to turnkey rental investing. Assume half of your rental income will be eaten up by costs and look at what the property now costs you. Like with house hacking, it's possible to have your home paid for by rental income. Typically, single-family homes offer great investment opportunities since they tend to be occupied for a long time. This is especially the case if the tenants are a newly married couple or have a young child. You're assured of them being in the neighborhood, barring unexpected circumstances, for at least 18 years. You can even pay off your mortgage early and act as a bank to them. Work out an interest rate and finance their property purchase. This will incentivize them to take care of the property, and you can earn a steady interest rate on your investment. Make sure you maintain the property and that you attract high-quality tenants. Other than that, turnkey rental investing is quite straightforward. You won't qualify for an FHA loan, so make sure your credit score is up to scratch since you'll need a traditional lender to approve you.

Flipping Properties

This is the strategy that most beginners think of when the topic of real estate investing comes up. However, it happens to be a pretty advanced method, and most beginners would not be able to execute it well. The typical property flip goes like this. The investor locates a property that needs fixing up. They estimate how much repairs the property needs and make an offer accordingly. They arrange financing and carry out the repairs. Once this is done, they either place the property back on the market for sale, or they rent it out and collect the cash flow every month. The exit strategy depends on the type of investor they are. A lot of home flippers look to maximize their cash on cash return and reinvest their money elsewhere. When planning exits, something to remember is FHA loans have a cooling-off period with regards to the sale of a property. This reduces the number of potential buyers. The average property that needs rehabbing isn't a multi-million dollar property. As a result, most potential buyers come with FHA financing. However, this risk is mitigated by simply placing the property on rent and then placing it back on sale in a year or so.

Most rehabbers have access to what is called the Multi Listing System or MLS. This is a network that is run by individual states, and it lists all of the properties that are up for sale in various counties. You need to be a real estate professional in order to get access to this network. In addition to this, you'll also need to pay fees every year for access. Experienced investors usually have a network of realtors who bring them properties the moment they hit the market. The key to success with rehabs is to beat the competition. Evaluating the repairs needed and figuring out the offer price is the key to success. Some experienced investors can simply look at photos and figure out how much repairs will cost and make an offer within an hour of the property arriving for sale on the market. This is why beginners will struggle with rehabbing properties. They lack a significant network, and as a result, only the worst properties remain on the market. These either require significant repairs or are the wrong kind of property that no one wants to buy.

Another hurdle is financing. Traditional lenders, including the FHA, don't finance rehabs. The FHA does have a 203(k) loan program that is aimed at low to moderate-income families. However, there is a primary residence requirement as with the traditional FHA mortgage. If you don't mind living in the property and house hacking it for a while, you can finance its purchase and repairs. Outside of the FHA, hard money lenders are the usual source of financing. Investors use bridge financing to finance the deal at first and then refinance using traditional mortgages once the property is occupied by tenants.

Appraisals of the property are extremely important. Most hard money lenders will loan you money on the basis of the ARV of the property. I've previously explained what ARV is. It's the value of the property once it's repaired fully. The ARV is also important when it comes to figuring out how much you need to offer on a property. This is where the 70% rule comes into play. The ideal offer price is calculated by subtracting the repair costs from the ARV. Now, take 70% of that number, and that's your offer price. This gives you a good margin of safety on the deal. The key to being a successful investor by rehabbing properties is to have good connections and a network you can rely on. Ideally, you'll have wholesalers, realtors, and contractors coming to you with potential deals. You'll need some input from the contractors to give you a rough idea of costs. Since they probably won't travel unless it's a job, you'll need to take good photos and show them the place so as to estimate repairs.

This concludes our look at investing in physical properties. There are a few more strategies you'll read about, but all of them involve a combination of these three basic strategies. The great thing about real estate is that these aren't the only ways of investing. You could invest in REITs, but there are a couple more ways to invest financially in real estate.

Financial Methods

By the term financial methods, I'm talking about not buying the property upfront. Instead, your aim is to invest a sum of money and then earn interest on it. There are two ways you can do this. The first is to invest in tax liens and deeds, and the other is to invest in mortgage notes.

Tax Lien Investing

Tax liens and deeds are a less known avenue of real estate investing. So what is a tax lien, and how does it differ from a deed? A tax lien is generated when a property owner doesn't pay their property tax. Counties rely on these taxes to keep things running smoothly. Once the property tax is overdue, the county typically auctions the lien to private investors. These auctions are conducted either online or in person. Smaller counties conduct in-person auctions due to there being a smaller number of properties available. The reason you won't see too many real estate investors attempting to purchase tax liens is due to the knowledge barrier.

The cost of investing in liens is quite low, usually less than $20,000, with the average purchase landing somewhere around $5,000. However, every state has a different method of dealing with the financial terms surrounding liens. For example, Texas has what's called a penalty system where the defaulter has to pay 25% of the lien as a penalty in the first year. If they fail to clear the debt in the first year, they'll pay 50% on the second year's debt. Georgia has a similar structure. Iowa doesn't have a penalty system but implements a fixed interest rate system. All counties in the state pay two percent per month in simple interest. Florida has a system where the interest is bid down on the property. Typically, you'll see Florida liens bid for a quarter percent. Why would anyone bid for such a low-interest rate? This is because Florida has a minimum penalty of five percent on outstanding liens. So no matter how low you go, you're going to get five percent a year.

Then there are tax deeds. States divide themselves between liens and deeds. In a deed auction, you're not bidding for the interest rate on the lien but on the property itself. It's exactly like a foreclosure auction. However, in a tax deed sale, the property owner can buy it back from you within a certain timeframe. If a lien or deed is defaulted on, you become the owner of the property. Here again, states deal with the process differently. Some states give you preference in terms of ownership, but some (such as Florida) pay you a maximum interest rate (18% in Florida's case) and place the property on auction. If all of this weren't confusing enough, there are different ways in which auctions are conducted. Some states conduct a bid down method where everyone bids a low-interest rate and the lowest wins. Others conduct a rotational bid where a property or lien is offered to everyone in turn. Some counties, especially smaller ones, will switch the auction method mid-way to get through the entire lot of liens being auctioned.

Liens are typically auctioned once every year in every state. Counties either conduct them on the same day or over a couple of weeks. Tax deed auctions happen regularly. You'll often find foreclosure investors hanging around here since these sales aren't as heavily advertised as regular foreclosures are. A lien or deed investment is a good way of earning a steady return on your money. Don't make the mistake of thinking it's a good way to luck into owning a great property. The odds of this happening are low. The good properties are usually snapped up by institutions. Individual investors are left with smaller properties. This doesn't mean they're bad. It's just that the amounts invested are smaller, and the rate of return isn't as attractive as on a physical real estate investment. If you happen to amass a large sum of money, you're probably better off investing in physical property. However, if you have $1,000 or $2,000 lying around, this is a good way to invest. Obviously, you won't be able to participate in tax deed auctions, but liens are open to you. For more information on this subject, check out Larry Loftus' book on the topic.

Mortgage Notes

What is the biggest hassle of physical real estate investment? It's the maintenance and constant checking up you need to do on your tenants. The property suffers from wear and tear, and you need to make sure it stays up to scratch. Mortgage note investing offers you a chance to become the bank in the property you invest in.

Banks typically do not want the hassle of having to maintain a property physically. Their job is to earn interest on their loans, and that's it. Maintaining properties and sourcing tenants is something they do not want to do, no matter how attractive the property might be.

Much like how counties get rid of liens they don't want by selling them to private investors, banks do the same. Except, they don't auction it in a public process. They instead sell them in batches to large institutional investors. However, not all of these mortgages are sold to institutions. Many make their way to private investors. So how does a mortgage note originate? The mortgage note is quite simply the mortgage on the property itself. When the owner defaults on their payment (doesn't pay for more than 90 days), this loan becomes a non-performing asset (NPA) on the bank's books. Banks hate NPAs since it represents dead money. Loan officers are evaluated on the basis of how many NPAs they generate every year. The lower, the better. Banks get rid of NPAs by either foreclosing on the property or selling the mortgage itself. Foreclosures are lengthy processes that take at least five to six months. The owner's rights need to be adhered to, and the courts get involved.

Typically, banks don't want to undertake all of this. They'd much rather offload the loan to someone else and get back to loaning to quality borrowers. A mortgage note sells for a heavily discounted price compared to the property's value as a result. While it might be unrealistic for you to buy notes from a bank such as Citibank, smaller banks are certainly open to working with individual investors. You'll need to project a professional demeanor and will need to indicate that you're serious about investing in notes. Something that makes it tough to deal with banks directly is that they expect investors to buy large batches of notes. This can easily run into six figures. Don't despair, though. You can buy mortgage notes in secondary markets. Websites such as Paperstac, Speed School, and Crexi.com have listings for mortgage notes on a large variety of properties. Speed School even offers an in-person course on the topic. Once you own the note, you technically own the property.

You can work out a payment plan with the owner of the property since you can provide them with more leeway than a bank can. If the owner continues to default, you can foreclose on the property and then resell it or lease it to a tenant. The thing to watch out for is the seniority of liens. The senior-most lien on a property happens to be the tax lien. If this is in default, you'll need to buy out the holder of the tax lien. Then comes any lien placed by the county. This is typically the case when the county carries out activities to make the property habitable once it gets abandoned.

Then comes the mortgage. Of course, properties can have more than one mortgage on them, so you'll need to check which note you're buying. The type of opportunities on offer can be pretty amazing. For example, right now on Paperstac, you can buy a performing first mortgage with the following terms:

- Unpaid balance - $5,500
- Interest rate - 10%
- Property value - $49,200
- Price of note - $4,500

A performing mortgage is one where the owner is making payments. The unpaid balance indicates how much is left of the original mortgage. The interest rate is what you'll be paid on the unpaid balance. Note that 10% of $5,500 is $550. However, you'll pay just $4,500. This means your true return is 12.2%. If the property owner defaults, you can foreclose and gain a property worth $49,200, having paid just $4,500 plus foreclosure fees. In this case, such a scenario is unlikely. However, it's a nice way to earn a high rate of return on your investment.

Crowdfunding

This chapter has given you a number of positive examples of real estate investment. Now for a negative one. Real estate crowdfunding has been hitting the headlines and has been presented as something revolutionary. However, it's something extremely unattractive dressed up as a revolutionary investment.

Here's how crowdfunding works. The company that invests in a real estate project sells units to individual investors and raises money to buy the property. The company then pays the investors their portion of rents and profits collected. Does this sound familiar? It should! It's exactly how a publicly traded REIT works. Why is a crowdfunded property a bad investment then? It has to do with the terms attached to the deal and the ease of exit. These crowdfunded investments are called eREITs. They are not traded on a public market, and this makes them tough to sell. If your investment starts going bad, you won't have any option but to sell to other holders of the eREIT or back to the company itself. This is not the case with a REIT that trades on a public stock exchange. You can always find someone to buy from you thanks to the massive number of market participants.

Then there are the terms. Most of these eREITs come with a lockup period. A lockup refers to how long your money needs to remain in the fund before you can withdraw your money. This is typically between six months to a year. Given that you can't exit easily to begin with, this is an absurd regulation. REITs don't have such terms and conditions placed on them. By investing in an eREIT, you're doing the following:

- Tying your money up in a small piece of real estate. Your money isn't diversified
- You cannot exit the investment easily

- You're forced to invest for a certain period of time

It's far better to invest in a publicly traded REIT. Stay away from these crowdfunded eREITs that use slick marketing to convince you to invest. This brings an end to our look at the world of real estate investment. Given the breadth of the topic, it's hard to cover all bases. My aim has been to give you a detailed overview of the many options available to you. Reread this chapter to understand the material better and dig deeper to better understand the ins and outs of how a particular method works. Take note that the financial methods require you to understand the legalese behind them. So don't rush into them by any means. Take your time understanding how they work.

Chapter 6:

Roth and Traditional IRAs

When it comes to passive income generation, opting to invest in an IRA is a no-brainer. IRA stands for individual retirement account, and there are different kinds of them. No matter the type, the benefits and features of IRAs are pretty much the same. The way they work is that you can contribute a certain sum of money every year and enjoy tax benefits. The kind of benefits you enjoy depends on the kind of IRA you're investing into. There are IRAs for people who work jobs as well as for those who are self-employed. You can either manage your IRA yourself or have someone else manage it for you. Typically, managers charge between one to 1.5% of your assets. Most people opt to hire a manager because they're afraid of going at it all alone.

As explained in the previous chapter on passive investing, you don't need to be afraid or intimidated by the stock market. All you need is a solid investment plan. You can use ETFs to design a good plan that will bring you a steady amount of gains over the long term. This is something you should keep in mind. An IRA is a tool you use for passive investment. It isn't meant to be used for active investment. Some people trade in and out of stocks in the IRA accounts with the reasoning that they'll achieve a number of tax benefits. While this might be true, remember that this is a retirement account and is meant to build your nest egg. Jumping in and out of the market with a get rich quick mindset is not what you want to do here. A key thing to understand with regards to contributions is that you can only deposit money that is considered earned income into an IRA. This is irrespective of the type of IRA you choose to form. The IRS defines just two ways in which an individual can earn earned income (*Earned Income | Internal Revenue Service*, 2020):

- By working for someone else
- By being self-employed and running a business or a farm

These are some the payments that qualify as earned income:

- Wages, salaries and tips
- Union strike benefits
- Disability retirement benefits received before retirement
- Earnings from your business
- Earnings obtained from being a member of a religious order

The following examples are instances of what does not qualify as earned income

https://www.irs.gov/credits-deductions/individuals/earned-income-tax-credit/earned-income:

- Pay received for work in a penal institution while an inmate
- Interest payments
- Dividend payments
- Pensions
- Annuities
- Unemployment benefits
- Child support
- Alimony
- Social security

You can open an IRA with any firm that is licensed and is regulated. Typical choices include a bank, a brokerage, or an investment firm. Now that this is clear, let's look at the different types of IRAs and how they work.

Traditional IRAs

A traditional IRA is the oldest form of a retirement account. The premise is quite simple. You can divert a portion of your pre-tax income into the IRA and invest it into any financial instrument of your choice. You can also invest in real estate and tax liens. The biggest advantage of the traditional IRA is that it's your pre-tax income that is being diverted. This means you get to compound a larger portion of your money. Your IRA contributions are tax-deductible, so it's a double benefit. The amount of money you can contribute to a traditional IRA depends on your age. If you're under 50, you can contribute $6,000 per year. Those over 50 can contribute $7,000 every year. The most complicated factor of traditional IRAs has to do with determining whether your contributions are tax-deductible or not. A lot depends on your modified adjusted gross income (MAGI). As long as your MAGI is below a certain limit, depending on your filing status, you can claim a deduction. Here are the limits for 2020 (Kagan, 2020):

- Single or head of household - $65,000
- If between $65,000 and $75,000 - partial deduction
- Greater than $75,000 - no deduction

- Married filing jointly - $104,000
- Between $104,000 and $124,000 - partial deduction
- Greater than $124,000 - no deduction
- Married filing separately - Less than $10,000 , partial deduction
- Greater than $10,000 - No deduction

IRA deposits can be withdrawn after the age of 59 ½. Upon withdrawal, you will have to pay taxes based on ordinary income earned. This is to say that you won't be paying capital gains taxes. The next chapter will help you understand the differences between these two. Generally speaking, capital gains taxes over the long term are always lower than ordinary income taxes. The question of whether your contributions will be tax-deductible also depends on whether you have other savings plans such as a 401(k) or 403(b) available at work. Consult a tax professional to determine what your exact situation will be. After the age of 72, you must begin to accept the required minimum distributions (RMD). The RMD is in place to stop people from using these accounts to avoid paying taxes.

Generally speaking, a penalty of 50% of the amount of the RMD is levied in case a person doesn't withdraw money. Determining the amount of the RMD is a bit complicated. The best way to calculate it is to use a calculator on your broker's website. You can find a good one at:

https://www.schwab.com/ira/understand-iras/ira-calculators/rmd.

Before the age of 59 ½, all withdrawals attract a 10% penalty rate over any taxes due. Given that these taxes are levied at the ordinary income rate, this is a hefty penalty indeed. It's best to leave these funds unattended for as long as possible so that they compound over time. This is why it's important to use only your post-tax income to budget for your living expenses.

Roth IRA

Unlike traditional IRAs, Roth IRA contributions are made with post-tax income. However, the huge advantage of Roth IRAs is that their distributions are tax-free. If you happen to realize huge capital gains or dividend income from your investments in the Roth IRA, these are not taxed once you withdraw them. This makes Roth a fantastic choice. In many cases, it makes more sense than a traditional IRA. Roth IRAs do not have any RMDs, and you can contribute to them as long as you have eligible earned income, irrespective of your age. In contrast, traditional IRAs have a contribution age limit of 59 ½. The contribution limits are the same as for traditional IRAs. However, there are income limitations to contributing to a Roth IRA. These MAGI limits are listed below (Kagan, 2020):

- Single or head of household - Less than $124,000 - Full contributions allowed
- Between $124,000 to $139,000 - Reduced amounts
- Greater than $139,000 - Zero contributions
- Married filing jointly - Less than $196,000 - Full contributions allowed
- Between $196,000 to $206,000 - Reduced amount
- Greater than $203,000 - Zero
- Married filing separately - Less than $10,000 - Reduced amount
- Greater than $10,000 - Zero

All regular Roth contributions must be made in cash (checks) and cannot be in the form of securities or assets. This is a major difference between this and a traditional IRA, where property can be held in a traditional IRA account. However, as long as you have a good plan of passive investment in the stock market, this isn't much of a limitation. A Roth IRA can be opened with any of the same institutions that offer regular IRAs such as banks, brokerages, or investment firms. When opening an account, make sure you read the IRA disclosure statement and the IRA adoption agreement and plan document. These explain the rules and regulations that govern the operation of the Roth IRA. They also establish an agreement between yourself and custodian of the IRA, which is the financial institution you open an account with. When choosing IRA providers, make sure you evaluate all of the investment options they offer you. Keep in mind that there might be additional fees that are charged to manage and operate your IRA.

The most common fee was the brokerage commission; however, these have been mostly done away with. The fees you'll incur are management fees or any fees related to the particular instruments you're investing in. For example, ETFs will attract a management fee. The institution will not charge a management fee unless you hire them to run your IRA. There are other miscellaneous fees to be aware of. Some providers cater to active traders and will charge you an inactivity fee if you don't place enough trades in a month. It's best to choose a provider who recommends passive investing since these accounts have the lowest fees involved. Some providers, such as Charles Schwab, etc., have minimum amounts that must be deposited in your IRA account. If you plan on banking with an institution, then it might make sense to tie all of your accounts together so that they're under the same roof.

A key point to remember is that IRAs, including Roth IRAs, are insured differently. Typically, a deposit account is insured for up to $100,000 by the Federal Deposit Insurance Corporation (FDIC). IRAs are insured for up to $250,000 by FDIC. However, this applies to combined IRA allowances. If you have a traditional IRA worth $100,000 and a Roth worth $100,000, you're insured fully. Anything over the combined limit is not insured. Also, your regular account balances are combined into this limit. If you have a certificate of deposit worth $100,000, then you're $50,000 over the limit, and this will not be insured. The Roth IRA has a subcategory called the spousal Roth IRA. You can fund a Roth IRA on behalf of your married partner who earns little or no income. These contributions are subject to the same rules and limits as regular IRA contributions are. It must be held separately from the Roth IRA of the individual making the contributions. In other words, these accounts cannot be combined. Here are the rules for making a spousal Roth IRA contribution:

- Couples must be married and file a joint tax return.
- The person making the contribution must do so from eligible earned income.
- The total contribution must not exceed taxable income filed on their joint tax return.

- Contributions to a single Roth IRA cannot exceed contribution limits. However, contributions to individual IRAs can be made at the specified limits.

Roth IRA withdrawals are tax and penalty-free as you've previously learned. This isn't as straightforward as it sounds, as is everything to do with taxation. First, a withdrawal that is equal to the amount of money you've contributed will not be considered as being subject to any penalty, irrespective of the age at which you withdraw the money. However, if you are withdrawing a sum greater than your contribution, you will pay a penalty of 10% if you do so before the age of 59 ½. The IRS calls this a qualified distribution. In addition to this, a qualified distribution is designated as such only if the withdrawal is made at least five years after your first contribution.

Here's the meaning of all this. You cannot withdraw funds without a penalty until you're 59 ½. The exception is if you're simply withdrawing what you deposited. In addition to this, your funds are effectively locked into the Roth IRA for a period of five years after your first contribution.

Lastly, qualified distributions must satisfy one of the following conditions:

- The distributions are used to purchase a first home for the holder of the IRA or a qualified family member. This is limited to $10,000 per lifetime.
- Distribution is made after the holder incurs a disability.
- Distribution occurs after the death of the IRA holder to a beneficiary.

Most people miss this part of the Roth IRA. While distributions are not taxable, you can withdraw it only after you're either disabled or after you're dead. Any contributions before this will attract income taxes.

Here are some of the non-qualified expenses:

- Unreimbursed medical expenses
- Medical insurance payments
- Higher education expenses (the exception is if it goes towards the owner's education or their dependents.)

- Childbirth or adoption expenses (the limit is $5,000 made within one year of the event.)

There is a loophole for the withdrawal of earnings. If you withdraw your entire contribution amount, including your earnings before the end of the tax year in which they were made, you won't have to pay taxes, irrespective of the reason for withdrawal. For example, if you invested $6,000 and earned a capital gain of $500 to bring the total value to $6,500, you can withdraw all of this tax-free before the tax year ends.

The Roth IRA is thus not necessarily better or worse than the traditional IRA. A lot depends on your tax bracket and on your income earned. In some cases, a traditional IRA is a better choice. You will pay taxes on the traditional IRA, but there is no limit on the reason for withdrawal. This isn't the case with a Roth IRA. If your withdrawals aren't qualified, you'll end up paying taxes twice, first on your contributions (since these are after-tax), and second upon withdrawal. On the flip side, Roth IRAs don't have RMDs, which gives you greater freedom when it comes to determining how to handle your cash.

Let's now move on and look at Simplified Employee Pension IRAs.

SEP IRAs

This IRA is a good choice for people, such as independent contractors, freelancers, and other small business owners. The idea behind introducing this type of IRA is that self-employed individuals have greater challenges when it comes to retirement planning. The traditional IRA contribution limits are too low and don't provide them with enough security. The SEP IRA has many features that are similar to a traditional IRA, but contains some additional features that make it a better plan. If you are self-employed in any way, you're eligible for a SEP IRA. These contributions are considered to be employer contributions. In essence, the business makes these contributions to you. You can contribute either 35% of your income or $57,000 yearly into this account. This isn't a Roth IRA, and there isn't any such option to convert it into one. The catch is that you must contribute an equal percentage of compensation for all other employees as well.

A SEP IRA can be opened with any financial provider. They're more advantageous than employer 401(k) plans that limit contributions to $19,500 yearly. You can take distributions after you're 59 ½ years old without attracting any penalties. Distributions taken prior to that will be penalized at 10%. There is an RMD requirement as well that kicks in after 72 years of age. Do note that even side hustle businesses allow you to open a SEP IRA. You can operate a regular retirement account such as a 401(k) at your day job and contribute even more money through the SEP IRA. As I mentioned earlier, if you happen to have a business with employees, then you'll need to contribute the same percentage of their income as you do to yours. The IRS defines the following people as qualified employees (Royal, 2020):

- People 21 and older
- Those who earn more than $600 annually
- Those who have worked at your business for the past three out of five years.

The question of matching contributions is problematic, and this is where a SIMPLE IRA offers advantages. You'll learn about this shortly. For now, understand that a SEP doesn't require you to contribute every year for either yourself or your employees. It's just that whenever you make a contribution, you'll need to contribute to your employees' retirement accounts as well. As a business owner, you can claim deductions on these contributions but only up to a certain limit. This depends on how your business is structured and on the other deductions you're claiming, so speak to a qualified accountant who will help you through this. The business as an entity is the one that can claim these benefits so it won't pass through to you always. Again, this depends on the structure of your business. Unlike traditional IRAs, there is no option for you to contribute a greater sum of money over the age of 50. With that in mind, the contribution limits are quite high, so this might not be a disadvantage.

SIMPLE IRA

SIMPLE stands for Savings Incentive Match Plan for Employees, and this is a traditional IRA that is available for small businesses and self-employed individuals. These contributions are tax-deductible, and you will pay taxes on your withdrawals over the age of 59 ½. They sound pretty similar to SEPs thus far. However, SIMPLE IRAs allow employees to make contributions. The employer is required to contribute to the employee's retirement account whether the employee contributes or not. This can be a dollar for dollar match of up to three percent of the employee's salary or a flat two percent of their salary. This means there is no need for you to contribute the same percentage or amount to your employees' accounts as you do for yourself. They have higher contribution limits than individual IRAs and are pretty easy to set up and run. There are a few caveats when it comes to setting it up, though. You must have 100 or fewer employees earning less than $5,000 every month. This includes all employees who have stopped working for you during the calendar year (not fiscal year).

The business cannot have any other plan other than a SIMPLE IRA. There are some exceptions to the contribution limits. For example, in two out of every five years, you can choose to lower your contribution to your employees to one or two percent of their compensation. SIMPLE IRAs are a lot easier to set up and administer compared to a

SEP IRA. The contribution limit for a year is $13,500, but there is a catch-up contribution. You can contribute $16,500 if you're over the age of 50. To choose the best IRA for yourself and your business, speak to a tax advisor to fully understand your options. The bottom line is that you must have money stored away in a retirement account at all costs.

Chapter 7:

Making Money Using ETFs

I've previously covered how ETFs work and how you can invest in them to turbocharge your passive investing results. In this chapter, I'm going to dive deeper into the types of ETFs available, what you should watch out for, and how taxation works on your market investments. You can make money using ETFs in active investment strategies, as well. However, given the hit or miss aspect of active strategies it makes sense for you to invest in a passive portfolio as a base before expanding to active strategies. There are different types of ETFs you can invest in. Broadly speaking, these are:

- Stock ETFs
- Bond ETFs
- Sector ETFs
- Commodity ETFs
- International ETFs

- REIT ETFs

Stock ETFs

These are the most common types of ETFs out there. Remember that an ETF can have any strategy and that the fund manager decides this. Some ETFs function as quasi hedge funds with high fees. They don't attract too much investment from the average investor, but they have large investor bases.

A stock ETFs portfolio mostly consists of stocks. A few ETFs contain other instruments such as bonds or short-term cash instruments such as certificates of deposit. It really depends on the manager's choice. The manager can also choose to redirect the fund's strategy at certain times, and this can jeopardize your investment. This typically never happens due to the manager realizing that doing this would mean the death of the fund. However, if times are desperate enough, fund managers can do this. I'd previously mentioned the case with an ETF that tracked the price of oil, where the managers changed the way the fund invested its money. Now that you understand how futures work a little bit better, you'll appreciate this story.

As the price of oil moved into negative territory, many investors jumped into U.S Oil, which is a huge ETF that tracks oil prices. Specifically, it tracks the prices of the West Texas Intermediate oil contract futures. The futures expiring in April moved into negative territory since oil supply was increasing, but demand dropped precipitously thanks to lockdowns happening everywhere. The price of the WTI April futures contract sank to -$40. U.S Oil was set up in such a way that it always rolled its positions over. When the April contracts would expire, the fund manager would simply roll the position over to May contracts. At that time, the May contracts were trading at a more sensible $12 or so. Many investors jumped in on U.S Oil thinking prices would jump from near single digits (the price of the ETF at the time) to $12 or so thanks to the change in price between the futures. They didn't take into account the fact that the ETF was hemorrhaging money thanks to the negative prices of oil in the market. As a result, it was losing money faster than investors could invest in it. Thus, the managers made a fateful decision to change the operating structure and to instead invest in a basket of futures contracts instead of just the next month's futures. This would result in the price of the ETF remaining around the same once the current month's contracts expired.

As a result of this change, the price of the ETF dropped by 30% since everyone sold the ETF. However, the fund managers thought it justified since the fund could at least survive and fight back once things normalized. The investors who placed their money in the fund without taking into account the vagaries of the oil market lost heavily, though. It just goes to show that when it comes to ETFs, you should do your research thoroughly. It isn't enough to understand just the ETF's structure but also the underlying market. This is why I recommended a passive investment portfolio using ETFs. Passive ETFs that track an index require very little work to maintain, and there's little that can go wrong with them. They're not trying to outperform the market using secret sauce and are not investing in complex derivatives like futures to track prices. Your risk is fully covered with them as a result.

Sector ETFs

These are a subset of equity ETFs and consist of stocks belonging to a certain sector. They can be diversified and also carry bonds and other instruments. It depends entirely on the kind of ETF portfolio the manager chooses to set up. Sector ETFs are a great way to invest in particular sectors of the economy without having to worry about conducting in-depth research into a particular company all by yourself. As always, make sure you read the fund prospectus and understand how the ETF is structured before investing in it.

REIT ETFs

Given that REITs are stocks, these are technically a subset of equity ETFs. These ETFs will pay you a handsome yield, and you'll earn pretty steady cash flow from them. You can choose to invest in a REIT fund that invests in REITs in a particular type of real estate or, you can choose a diversified REIT.

Bond ETFs

These are the second most popular type of ETF available on the market. Bond ETFs track bonds or bond indexes and are a good choice for a passive investment strategy. Keep in mind that just because the ETF tracks a bond, this doesn't mean it's a safe investment. Bond ETFs can also be leveraged and inverse as with stocks. They aren't as prevalent since it's much tougher to short a bond than it is a stock. In fact, in order to short a bond, these funds need to invest in derivatives that move in opposite directions to bonds. This, of course, increases the complexity that is inherent in these funds. As a result, the average investor is best served by staying away from such ETFs. In fact, a few of these ETFs are fronts for hedge funds who need someone to take the other side of their trades.

The market is pretty simple when you get down to it. If you buy something, someone else is selling it to you. If you make money, someone else is losing money. Suppose a hedge fund wishes to place a bet on a certain basket of bonds but can't find anyone to take the other side of their trade. The investment bank that acts as their broker might create an ETF. This ETF is then marketed to ordinary investors; as a result, the hedge fund receives a number of smaller traders who they can trade against. When the time comes to exit these ETFs, you'll find a very small market for them and will likely be gouged when you try to get a good price for them. Play it safe when it comes to ETFs. Many investors think all ETFs are safe, but clearly, this isn't the case.

Commodity ETFs

These ETFs function a lot like U.S Oil does and track the prices of commodities. However, the way they track them and the methods they use to determine their prices vary. For example, you can buy ETFs that track the prices of gold futures directly. However, there are also ETFs that invest in gold mining companies and other companies that profit from the gold prices. The same case occurs with silver. Silver is often used as industrial raw material, and as a result, the ETFs tracking silver have a wide variety of ways in which they track the prices of the metal. Make sure you read the prospectus thoroughly and understand how the manager operates their fund. At the end of the day, you don't have much control over how the fund operates. Like with U.S Oil, you could end up in a bad situation.

For this reason, it's best to buy the futures for yourself or to invest in individual stocks instead of relying on an ETF. Commodities are not passive investments and move in economic cycles of their own. As a result, you'll be exposing yourself to huge amounts of risk if you simply leave your investment without monitoring the underlying market.

International ETFs

I've already explained why international stocks and funds that track them are risky propositions. Over the years, many economies and countries have been touted as being the next superpower. Only China has fulfilled this promise with every other country eventually keeling over. It's best to stay away from these.

Taxation

Taxes are an unavoidable expense in investing and passive income generation. The best you can do is minimize them. To minimize them, you need to understand how they work. Thankfully, this isn't a tough task. There are three kinds of taxes you will incur: Long term capital gains taxes, short term capital gains taxes, and ordinary income taxes. Short term capital gains taxes are the same as ordinary income taxes. When you receive your salary, you pay a certain amount of it as taxes.

This amount is determined by the amount of money you make, and you'll be taxed according to certain brackets. The tax you pay depends on how you file as well. Here is a brief rundown of how the tax brackets are divided (El-Sibaie, 2019):

- 10% taxes
    - Single filers- Income over $0
    - Married couples - Income over $0
    - Heads of households - Income over $0
- 12% taxes
    - Single filers- Income over $9,875
    - Married couples - Income over $19,750
    - Heads of households - Income over $14,100
- 22% taxes
    - Single filers- Income over $40,125
    - Married couples - Income over $80,250
    - Heads of households - Income over $53,700
- 24% taxes
    - Single filers- Income over $85,525
    - Married couples - Income over $171,050
    - Heads of households - Income over $85,500
- 32% taxes
    - Single filers- Income over $163,300
    - Married couples - Income over $326,600
    - Heads of households - Income over $163,300
- 35% taxes
    - Single filers- Income over $207,350
    - Married couples - Income over $414,700
    - Heads of households - Income over $207,350
- 37% taxes
    - Single filers- Income over $518,400
    - Married couples - Income over $622,050
    - Heads of households - Income over $518,400

Note that these brackets are progressive. If you earn $100,000, the first $9,875 is taxed at 10%, the next $40,125 is taxed at 12% and so on.

Thus the real tax rate you pay will vary. Short term capital gains are treated in the same way.

What is a capital gain, and how is its term determined? Capital gains occur when you sell an asset for a price greater than what you bought it for. If you sell the asset less than a year after you bought it, this is a short term gain. An asset sold after holding onto it for more than a calendar year is a long term capital gain. Long term capital gains taxes are lower than ordinary income taxes. The tax you pay depends on your tax bracket. Here's how they're taxed:

- 0%
    - Single - $0
    - Married - $0
    - Heads of households- $0
- 15%
    - Single - $40,000
    - Married - $80,000
    - Heads of households- $53,600
- 20%
    - Single - $441,450
    - Married - $496,600
    - Heads of households- $469,050

Given that the maximum capital gains taxes you'll pay is 20%, it makes a lot of sense to hang onto your investments for as long as possible.

Dividend and interest income is taxed at ordinary income tax rates. If you invest in mortgage notes, for example, and receive interest payments form the homeowner, you'll have to pay taxes at ordinary income tax rates. When it comes to dividends, things get a bit more complex.

Dividend Taxation

Dividends for the purposes of this discussion is any cash distribution you receive from an ETF or a common stock. Distributions from bond funds also come under this category. There are two buckets into which dividend payments are split. The first is qualified dividends, and the second is ordinary dividends. Ordinary dividends are taxed as ordinary income. Qualified dividends are treated as capital gains. The length of time you've held your investment determines whether you'll pay long term or short term capital gains taxes. When determining the tax rate, you'll be charged your dividend income will be added to the rest of your capital gains and ordinary income, and you'll pay taxes accordingly. You don't need to worry too much about determining how much of your dividends are ordinary versus capital gains. Your broker will issue a form called the 1099-DIV, which will clearly specify how much of your dividend income was ordinary versus qualified. You need to use this information when filing your taxes at the end of the year. This applies to all dividends except REIT dividends. Given that these are real estate dividends, they're treated a bit differently.

REIT Dividend Taxation

REIT dividends are also divided into two categories. These are ordinary income and return of capital (ROC). Ordinary income is treated the same way as mentioned before. ROC is a different beast, though. This is treated as capital gains. However, the taxes on them are deferred.

The IRS considers ROC as a reduction in the cost basis of your investment. Let's say you bought a REIT for $100 per share and received a ROC payment of $1. According to the IRS, your effective purchase price is now $99, not $100. When you sell the investment, your capital gains will be calculated on the adjusted cost basis rather than the actual cost you paid. If the REIT sells for $120, your profit, according to the IRS, isn't $20 per share (bought at $100 and sold at $120) but $21 (sold at $120 and bought at $99). The thing about ROC is that you'll pay taxes on it only when you sell your investment. If you happen to hold onto your investment till you die, you don't need to pay ROC taxes. At some point, ROC might even reduce your cost basis to zero. Once this happens, any ROC you earn from that point on is taxed at long term capital gains rates. You can pass your investment holdings onto your heirs. Once you do this, their cost basis is readjusted to the level it was on the date of your demise. Thus, the ROC they earn from that point on will continue to reduce their cost basis.

The pertinent question is, how is the division between ROC and ordinary income determined? This is done automatically by the IRS and your broker. The full explanation requires an understanding of accounting principles in the United States, so I'm not going to bore you with that. If you are interested, read the italicized paragraph below. The ordinary income component is equal to the net income, as declared by the REIT, in its financial statements. ROC is any dividend payment that is in excess of net income. For example, if the REIT declares $1.20 of net income, and pays $3.00 as dividends, ordinary dividends are $1.20, and ROC is $1.80.

For those of you interested in accounting principles, Generally Accepted Accounting Principles (GAAP) states that a company must depreciate its assets. In the case of a REIT, it's assets are physical properties. However, real estate appreciates over time if it's well maintained. Depreciation, therefore, isn't a real expense. However, they need to account for it under GAAP, and this is why REIT dividend payments often exceed declared net income. Pay attention to the cash flow instead of net income when analyzing a REIT.

This is a simple illustration of why it's best to buy a diversified REIT ETF and hang onto it for as long as possible. You'll be paid to hold onto your investment, and you won't have to ever pay capital gains taxes on it potentially. Do keep in mind that you'll still be on the hook for these taxes if you opt for a DRIP. Some people forget about DRIPs since they never see the income enter their accounts as cash. However, you'll still need to pay taxes on them.

Physical Real Estate Taxes

One of the biggest benefits of owning physical real estate is that you can deduct a large number of taxes. You can deduct your mortgage interest payments, depreciation (which is the amount of wear and tear your property absorbs over a year), mortgage insurance, and so on. Compiling these taxes by yourself might be intimidating, so it's best to maintain receipts of everything you did throughout the year and submit these to your accountant.

Chapter 8:

Profitable Passive Income Models Outside of Real Estate and the Markets

The internet's explosion has meant that starting a side business is now easier than ever. The way the internet works also makes it easy to create passive income businesses. These businesses require initial work, and you can then let them go away and create income for you. As long as you maintain them from time to time, you'll be able to ensure a fully passive income stream. These business models all depend on the internet, but they're different in terms of execution. Like with real estate investment methods, you can combine them to create a large income stream. In fact, some of the most successful online businesses do this. Let's dive in and look at some of the most profitable business models. I'd like to point out that there is a difference between a business model and the way you monetize the business. For example, content creation (which you'll learn about next) is a business model. You can choose any number of monetization methods to earn money from it. Keep this in mind as you read through this chapter.

Content Creation

Content creation in the earlier days of the internet used to mean starting a blog about a topic and writing stuff. These days, there's no limit to the kind of content you can create. You can write blogs, newsletters, create videos, create stories, webinars, host virtual summits, and so on. The kind of content you can create is also unlimited. For example, an Instagram profile is a form of content creation. Many people who begin their internet business journey think about content in terms of what people find useful. This isn't entirely true. It's more about what people want to consume. For example, Vine and its successor TikTok are full of young people dancing to popular songs. There's no conceivable utility in this form of content, but it brings a massive number of eyeballs. This highlights a singular truth about all online businesses. As long as you can generate traffic, you can potentially monetize it. No one cares how you generate traffic.

This is why people go to extreme lengths to generate attention. It's up to you whether you want to go about this positively or negatively. Generate enough attention, and you can even get elected President! Here are some of the best platforms for you to create content on right now:

- YouTube
- Blogs
- WordPress, Squarespace, Wix, Weebly
- Pinterest
- Instagram
- TikTok
- Twitch
- LinkedIn

Each of these mediums has its own quirks and audience. YouTube is the second-largest search engine in the world and is host to a wide variety of topics. You can create a channel around pretty much anything, and as long as you post consistently, you can gain traffic. Blogs are the oldest way of creating content, and these days it takes a while to rise up in Google search engine result rankings. The names I've mentioned in the list are platforms that allow you to create great looking websites. If you're creating content on blogs, then you must also create content on at least two other mediums in the list above. This will help you rise in the rankings a lot faster. Pinterest is a visual search engine that is gaining ground on Google with regards to image search. The great thing about Pinterest is that it hosts content on a wide variety of topics, and you can link to your website directly from your content. The platform is pushing paid search increasingly these days, but organic reach remains high. Organic reach refers to the number of users your content reaches without you having to pay for it. Facebook ranks dead last when it comes to organic content reach. If you have 1,000 friends on your profile, it doesn't matter. Facebook will show your posts to just a handful of accounts.

The platforms listed above have high levels of organic reach, and this is why I recommend you create content on them. After Pinterest, we have Instagram. This is a great platform for gaining attention thanks to its visual medium. It doesn't cater to every kind of content. For example, anything related to male fitness isn't going to do well since this doesn't translate well to a visual medium. However, you can build an audience relatively quickly on the platform. Facebook hasn't completely turned this into a paid ads platform, so there's still a lot of opportunity. TikTok and Twitch audiences are younger. TikTok hosts the kind of content I mentioned previously, and Twitch is a gamer's paradise. Twitch streams are some of the most popular types of content right now, and if you love playing games, then this is a great way for you to build an audience.

On the other extreme is LinkedIn. No one really talks about LinkedIn when it comes to content creation or business, but it's extremely powerful if you want to build a professional profile or conduct B2B selling (B2B is business to business and refers to products that businesses buy. This is opposed to business to consumer models such as Amazon). People respond to LinkedIn mails and messages at a far higher rate than emails, and it's a great platform to spread the word about your business. You will need to be professional on the network and conduct yourself in a certain manner. Do this well, and you'll grow your business immediately.

Notice that I haven't mentioned anything about earning money as yet. This is because when it comes to online content creation (or any online business), you need to first focus on getting as much traffic as possible. You can be an idiot and generate traffic. However, unless you happen to be one for real, it's tough to sustain this interest. Therefore, the best way to generate traffic is to provide value. As long as you give people what they want (not what you think they want), you'll build a good amount of interest and create a loyal audience. So how do you go about creating a large audience? The first step is to select a niche.

Niche Selection

Niche selection is the most important part of your content creation plan. You need to match what people want to consume to what you can create. Most people make the mistake of jumping into creating content centered around the most popular monetization models or the most popular niches. This is a mistake. Once again, I'd like to remind you that I haven't mentioned anything about monetization at this point. Your sole focus should be on creating quality content. So what are the things you're interested about? What can you talk about for hours without taking a break? A good test to apply here is to ask yourself whether you can talk about something and create content around it for at least three years. Do you know enough about it, and can you keep creating content even when no one is watching you? If the answer is no, move onto the next business model.

Remember that content creation doesn't necessarily mean blog content or videos. It can also be an Instagram profile or Pinterest boards. You can create content without the help of a website or a channel. Instagram and Pinterest require you to create visually appealing images. As long as your pictures look good, you'll generate interest. I'd like to mention that you need a website to monetize your business model. Therefore you must plan on getting one at some point. However, you don't need this in the beginning. A good niche for you might even be something you're willing to research into. For example, if you're really into dirt bikes and are looking at getting into it, start a blog documenting your journey.

The only exception to this is cooking and personal finance. Cooking is an extremely crowded niche, and it heavily favors the early movers. People who started blogs a long time back are well entrenched, and it's hard to compete. Personal finance and anything to do with health or legal issues are treated seriously by Google. If you don't have credentials or some authority in the space, your content will not rank in Google. If you do have credentials (CFA, CPA, any medical licenses, etc.), then display them prominently on your website. There are a large number of niches out there. However, matching what you find interesting to what people find interesting is a tough thing to do. In fact, most people are not suited for content creation. This isn't a bad thing since there are other business models for you to explore. Just because you can't write about something everyone is interested in doesn't mean you can't create an online income. Assuming you find a niche you'd like to write about, how do you decide what content to create?

Choosing Topics

The term "topic" isn't the same as niche, so do keep that in mind. Topic refers to the things you'll be creating content around. If you happen to know the niche well, this shouldn't be an issue. The question is whether these things are what your audience is searching for. There are multiple ways you can go about doing this. The easiest way is to use Google's keyword tool. This is available for free use once you spend a few dollars on Google Ads. You can spend as little as a few cents and start using the tool. Take the results with a grain of salt. The tool is used by advertisers to determine which keyword phrases are the best to target. The monthly keyword search volume can be a bit misleading at times. However, it gives you a good idea of what people are searching for. Look for keywords that are at least three words long and are being searched over 1,000 times per month. The higher the number of searches, the better. The tool gives you keyword suggestions, so use these as well to find even more keywords. You'll have a decent list of them by now. Don't start creating content yet! It's time to gather even more keywords and to figure out search intent.

Search intent is the process of uncovering what your audience is really searching for. For example, a search term like "is crowdfunding good?" can contain multiple intents. The user might be asking, "is crowdfunding good for small business?" "Is crowdfunding a good option for me?" "Is crowdfunding successful?" "Is crowdfunding useful to raise funds for charity?" and so on. Determining this isn't always easy, but Google helps you out with this. The way to do this is to search for the keyword phrase in Google and look at what comes up. It'll be pretty easy to figure out what the results are trying to communicate. If you see a common theme amongst all of the results in terms of intent, then Google is telling you exactly what your audience's intent is. If you can't spot a firm theme and if the results are covering multiple intents, then even Google isn't sure. This is a great opportunity for you to create great content and get ranked faster. The previous case also presents an opportunity, but your content will have to be of a higher quality than the highest-ranked post.

Another way to figure out intent and to structure your content is to look at the questions that Google displays in between the results. Google isn't displaying these by accident. They have more data than anyone else in the world (save for the Chinese government). They've seen the patterns and know that these questions are helpful to their users. Structure your content in a way so as to cover all of these questions, and you'll help your audience even more.

Lastly, look at the related search terms at the bottom of the first page. These are similar to the questions displayed and will give you even more keywords. Lastly, use the alphabet soup method. Type a term related to your niche and add "a" after it. Google will give you suggestions and results. Note down all of these. Next, add "b" after your niche term and repeat the process. Work your way to "z," and you'll have a large list of topics to cover. Repeat the process with the additional keywords you generated, and you'll have no problems figuring out what content to create for the next few months at the very least.

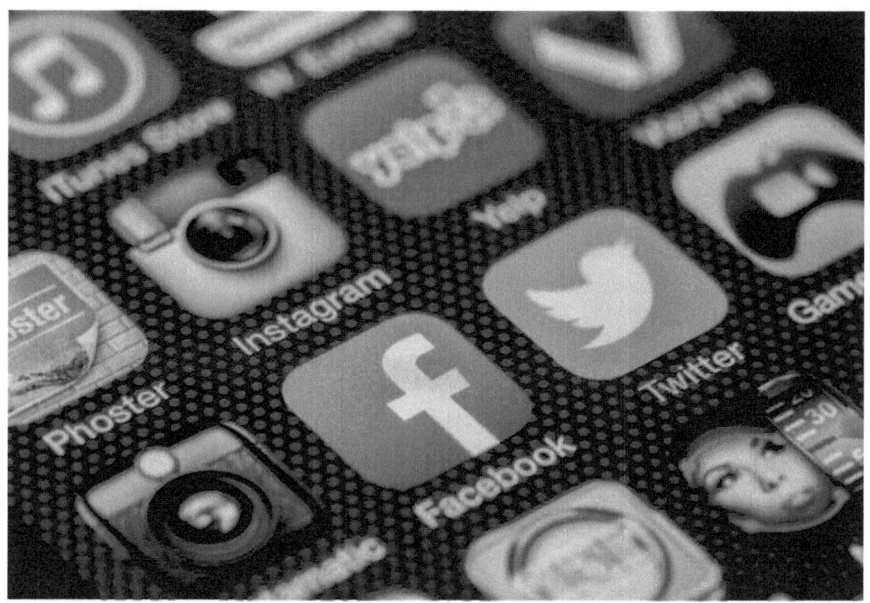

I must mention that this method won't work for social media platforms such as TikTok and Instagram. These are visually-driven platforms, but it's easy to figure out what the successful accounts are doing. The key is to look at accounts that are slightly bigger than yours. If you have 1,000 followers, look at what a 5,000 follower account is doing. It doesn't make sense to copy the hashtags and post styles of a million follower account.

TikTok is a relatively new platform, so there isn't a firm strategy as yet. However, you can apply the same principles. The methods might be different, but remember the theme behind all of this: You want to create content that your audience wants to consume. Don't think you can force content down their throats just because you think it's best for them. You can do that only after you've attained a certain size and level of influence in your niche.

YouTube keyword research follows the exact process as described above with an additional step. Use YouTube suggestions and look at the types of videos being created in your niche. Pay attention to the number of views the videos are receiving and which topics seem to be getting the lion's share of views. Look at the related videos playlist on the right-hand side (bottom on mobile) and comb those for even more topics. The related videos playlist is a goldmine to discover topics and angles that you can cover. For example, the same topic might be covered differently by content creators. This shows you what's working.

Topic research is time-consuming. The good news is you need to do this only once or twice at the most. Once you begin creating content on a regular schedule, you'll start noticing what works and what doesn't. Topics will automatically suggest themselves to you, and you'll create even more content, over and above what you're already doing. The key is to give your audience what they want. Schedule content creation using a calendar and stick to it. You don't have to create content every single day. Instead, follow a schedule and stick to it. This is especially true for YouTube. Once you get comfortable recording videos of yourself, you can record seven or eight of them in a day and release two every week. This way, you're covered for a month in advance. If any topic suggests itself to you in between, you can always create a short video around it. Don't worry too much about video length and so on. Just make sure your content is at least one percent better than what's out there. If you can't do this, then you don't stand a chance, unfortunately. The same applies to blog posts as well. Many content creators get stuck on search engine optimization and all of this. You don't need to worry about these things. If your content is great, people will come to you. Google and YouTube will reward you for great content. The same applies to Instagram and TikTok like platforms.

Boosting Traffic

Once you've published content and are creating it steadily, you can sit back and wait for traffic to roll in, or you can be more proactive about it. A metric that Google values is backlinks. Backlinks are links that other content creators have placed on their channels that link to you. The higher quality your backlinks are, the more authority you have in your niche. Google notices this and rewards you with traffic. Backlinks have come a long way since the early days of the internet when you could toss them around in forums and comment sections. These days Google penalizes you for doing this, not to mention you'll upset people who run these channels. What you need to do is reach out to blog owners and provide value. You could suggest a topic that is relevant to your niche or offer your spin on it that contradicts current wisdom. The issue is that many popular blog owners are inundated with such requests. So how can you break in?

One method is to flatter them. You could take their advice on a topic and put it into practice. Document your results and then reach out to them and let them know about it. This will organically lead to a blog post request. Alternatively, you could publish a post on your blog or create a video around it and let them know. Everyone likes being flattered as long as it's sincere. Another method is to suggest a collaboration. These people might be too busy to experiment with something in their niche. Suggest that you could do the work for them and add their name to the case study while using their inputs periodically. The published study will boost their credibility, and they'll be happy to link back to your blog. At the end of the day, you need to provide value. Make sure you do this, and you'll receive backlinks.

Another way of boosting your traffic is to expand across different channels. If you're only on YouTube, start writing blog posts. If you're only writing blogs, start recording videos. Create infographics on Pinterest using tools like Canva. Content creation of this sort should come easily to you since you'll simply have to translate one medium into another. You don't have to write blogs if you don't enjoy them. However, it's best to expand to at least one other social media channel. Instagram is not a channel to expand into unless you know how to grow your account. Pinterest has high rates of organic reach, and this is why it's a great option. Don't bother creating anything on Facebook. Content creators usually hit dead ends on that platform. It's far better to focus on other media channels.

Nurture

Once all of the above tasks have been completed, you'll start seeing some traffic regularly. You might not receive large numbers, but you should still execute one very important step. You need to build a community. This alone will ensure people keep coming back to you. You want to frame yourself and your readers as being a part of a journey or a quest to discover something. It could also be something like making the world a better place, and so on. The point is to connect emotionally with your audience and to not view them as being mere bags of money (which they are, but we're not there yet in the process.) Some content creators do this by hosting Facebook groups. These take some effort in terms of moderation and content curation. You want your audience to create their own content in here and share success stories etc. Slack is another great tool to use to build a community. In fact, Slack is a better option since the platform allows you to own all information about your audience.

This is critical because you'll have to start collecting email addresses at this point. Your email list is a valuable asset, and you should treat it as such. You should run email newsletters to your audience with the aim of nurturing your community. Involve them in your content decisions by creating polls and asking them for feedback. You don't need to send more than one newsletter per week. Focus on creating great content instead, and people will come to you. At some point, you'll realize that your community trusts you and that you're receiving pretty high levels of traffic. Finally, it's time to monetize.

Monetization

The first method of monetization is ad placement. You can run ads on your website and get paid for every click. Ad networks prefer content channels that attract a specific group of people. The only exception is if your website or channel is as big as CNN or some news outlet. The ad network everyone gets started out with is Google AdSense. This allows you to monetize YouTube as well, but the video platform has certain criteria that need to be met. You can read these at:

https://support.google.com/youtube/answer/1311392?hl=en.

AdSense for blogs doesn't have such restrictions, but it helps to have good audience numbers. At the very least, if you're receiving 5,000 unique visits every month, this is a good number. The larger your unique visits are, the more you can potentially earn. You can sign up for higher-paying ad networks such as Ezoic. Keep in mind that the ad networks prioritize user experience, so you need to be careful with ad placement. The higher paying networks also require you to have certain audience visit numbers. Some content creators choose to skip monetization with ads because of decreased user experience. This decision is entirely up to you. It's a great source of passive income since you do nothing differently.

There are other means of monetizing your website. A popular route is to create an informational or info product. This could be a course, an ebook, or a consulting service that you could launch. Your choice will depend on your niche, of course. Certain niches lend themselves very well to all three avenues. You can host your course on websites such as Udemy, Skillshare, or Teachable and create modules for your audience to follow. You can sell your ebook directly through your website or sell it through Amazon's KDP service. This allows you to sell your book in paperback and audiobook format as well. A consulting service could be a program, and you could sell it in monthly packages. If you're in the health and fitness niche, you could sell monthly subscriptions to workouts or meal plans and so on. The choices are endless. Selling subscriptions is a great way to ensure steady cash flow and to lock in your users for at least a year.

Another way of monetizing your website is through affiliate marketing. Affiliate marketing is a way for you to earn a commission on the sale of a product. Think of yourself as being a salesperson. Whenever you send someone to buy a product, you get paid a commission. You can sell pretty much anything via affiliate marketing. Courses, products, subscriptions, you name it. You can find popular affiliate products on marketplaces such as Clickbank, CJ, and Amazon Associates. Amazon is quite popular with lots of people, but since they're a big company, you're not in control of anything. They could, and will slash commissions whenever they feel like it.

A final option to monetize your audience is to sell print on demand products such as apparel, pillows, and so on. You can use services such as Printful or Teespring to do this. These companies print and ship your products and pay you cash every month. You could also integrate an e-commerce store on your website where you sell your own products. This ties into the dropshipping business model, which you'll learn next.

Dropshipping and E-Commerce

Starting an online store to sell stuff has never been easier. You don't need to worry about creating your own store online. You can simply signup for a service like Shopify or WooCommerce and have a fully built store ready to go in a few minutes. However, building a store is the easy bit. Ensuring you're selling the right products is another task entirely. The fact is that despite the growth in people's willingness to buy products online, many products sell better offline. For example, large furniture pieces almost never sell online, because people like sitting in them and trying them out.

The same behavior applies to mattresses and vehicles. Most dropshipping advice tells you to pick a big-ticket item, but there aren't many that you can actually sell. The typical dropshipper this ends up selling cheaply made small items sourced from China. However, doing this is a bad move as well since it doesn't provide your customer with any value. The biggest hurdle you need to cross with dropshipping and e-commerce is shipping time. Although the rest of the world has moved forward, logistics remain in the 1800s. Packages are still delivered by trucks and are manually sorted in warehouses. Your average courier service is prone to losing packages in shipment and misplacing or damaging items. These are problems you'll deal with later. The place to begin with is once again niche selection. To be more precise, your aim should be product selection. The idea is to figure out what people are buying a lot of online and sell it to them. The good thing with products is that they're tangible things.

You don't need to spend time figuring out search intent. Instead, you can see what they want and sell it to them. The first step is to head over to Amazon. It's the world's largest e-commerce store and offers a ton of valuable data. Amazon displays a valuable metric called the best seller's rank or BSR. The lower a product's BSR is, the better it sells. There's no direct way to measure sales based on BSR numbers. You can use tools such as Jungle Scout's BSR to sales estimator to figure out how much revenue a product generates.

Begin by visiting Amazon's bestseller lists and looking at products that are selling well. Stay away from books and such. You want to find products. This could be anything from apparel to toys to pet products, and so on. You'll see a lot of branded products there, so stay away from these. For example, Nike shoes sell really well, but you don't want to compete against them for obvious reasons. Look for products that you can replicate for yourself. Hobby niches offer great opportunities as do niches containing products that aren't brand dependent. For example, people don't really care what sort of cookware they use. As long as it's safe, they'll buy it. Some electronics such as smartwatches or fitness trackers also fall into this category. Electronics are tricky things to sell, so make sure the product is as simple to design as possible. You want your product to be priced above at least $20. This gives you enough margin to make a profit. You'll have a list of products that match your criteria. Now, it's time to head over to Google and see whether people are searching for them.

Evaluating Demand

You want products that have innate demand. Google's keyword tool offers the best insights into this. Look at monthly search volume for the keywords related to the product. Volumes greater than 1,000 every month indicate a good number of searches. Your next step is to figure out how you want to sell your product. You could sell it one time, but you could also design a subscription-based model around it. For example, a lot of personal care brands sell subscription boxes with a variety of products in them. This helps maintain customer relationships. The company selling these boxes end up earning more money than they would on a single sale. Check out the Google reviews of existing products. These are your competitors, so take note of the product's flaws and how they can be improved. These are great design ideas for you to explore. Once you've narrowed your list down to a few products, it's time to test demand.

The easiest way to do this is to set up a dummy website using WordPress or Wix and then post pictures of your chosen product. You don't have the product in stock as yet, so you can't offer checkout services. Instead, your objective is to measure how many people click the checkout button. Once they click this button, you can display a popup that says you don't have the item in stock and you can notify them when it becomes available. Capture their email in a form for this purpose. How do you drive traffic to this dummy website, though? You do this by running Google ads. Run simple search term ads and spend less than $50 on testing. Look at how many clicks it takes you to get a single "checkout" click. If the product gives you a profit after a $50 ad spend, it's a winner—obviously, the greater your profit, the better.

You can play around with the pricing of your product and see how well it sells. Typically, you can price it for the same as your competitors and estimate your profits. You can estimate product prices by looking it up on supplier websites such as Alibaba or AliExpress. I must stress the importance of running Google ads and not Facebook ads. Facebook touts its targeting system, but in reality, these aren't great for testing products. The company is far more concerned with squeezing money out of advertisers than providing any value. Once you have a winner, it's time to examine product sourcing.

Sourcing and Supply

This is the most important aspect of your business. You need to find a good manufacturer who can create a great product for you and reliably handle shipping. The problem is that great manufacturers don't often handle shipping. They outsource this to fulfillment agents. These agents run warehouses where your product is stored and shipped to your customer. They offer a backend integration to your website that will allow you to track shipments and inventory. However, we're not there yet. At this point, you don't have a website.

You should locate manufacturers that are as close to your customers as possible. If your product happens to be small such as wallets or kitchen utensils, you can get away with sourcing everything from China. However, if your product is slightly bulky and requires assembly, it's best to locate your manufacturer as close to your customer as possible. Mexico, Eastern Europe, and China offer great locations for factories producing goods. The typical dropshipper automatically chooses China since they don't expand past AliExpress. You need to speak to the manufacturer over the phone and even visit them if possible. This way, you can assess their production capabilities.

You need to strike a balance between being their only customer and being one of many. The ideal situation is when you're one of their top two customers, but they have other smaller orders bringing them income. This way, you'll be treated with priority, and you can ensure your product reaches your customers on time. Discuss branding and other custom requirements with them and negotiate a price. Some factories will require you to order a minimum quantity upfront. Don't fall for this. Instead, tell them you'd like to order five or 10 samples first to evaluate their production quality. The manufacturer knows what's going on, but they can hardly say no to this. Collect your samples and move onto the next phase of your plan.

Crowdfund

One of the biggest issues with selling physical products is that you need to invest a lot of money upfront. What if your product fails? You've tested demand previously, but what if there's some other issue that crops up? To avoid this, crowdfunding your product is best. This allows people to preorder your product, and you'll receive the money upfront before having to pay your manufacturer. Your customers will pay you to manufacture your product. The best way to drive traffic to your campaign is to reach out to influencers and send them a sample of your product. Notify them of when you're going live with your product and tell them to drop their review at that time. Launch your campaign on Kickstarter and set a reasonable funding goal. It's best to set this equal to your minimum quantity as required by your manufacturer.

If your product is good, you'll exceed this goal many times over (assuming the minimum quantity is reasonable). You can create YouTube videos of your product and start social media channels of your own. Additionally, you can hire agencies to help promote your product for a fee. Build out your website and other channels to handle the incoming orders. Remember that there's a good chance of your campaign succeeding thanks to the previous steps you've taken. Once it's finished, place the order with your manufacturer and start delivering products to your customers. Make sure you encourage them to visit your website. You'll collect their emails during the crowdfunding process so you'll have a good database of customers. And that's how you'll earn your initial profit!

Scaling Your Business

Scaling your business is the best way to multiply your profits. The first step is to sell in international markets such as Europe. Next, use the emails you've collected to create lookalike audiences on Facebook. This will double your sales at the very least. You can run product shopping ads on Google and even sell on Amazon using Fulfilled by Amazon (FBA). Under the FBA model, you send your products to Amazon's warehouses, and they take care of everything else. Apply these methods gradually, and you'll end up quadrupling your sales. Down the road you could add more products that compliment your primary product or create an improved version.

Self-Publishing

Self-publishing is a great way to earn some income on the side. You can run this business as a side hustle or as a full-fledged publishing company. The key here is to drive traffic to your book. You can use Amazon's ads system to do this or use influencer marketing tactics to do so. One business model is to hire ghostwriters to create books on a topic for you and then contact influencers to review your book on their channels. This brings traffic to your product page. Amazon makes it really easy for you to create paperback and audiobook versions of your book. Once published, you earn royalties from the book in perpetuity. The Kindle Direct Publishing (KDP) interface is quite straightforward to use. Amazon uses ACX (which is Audiobook Creation Exchange) to create audiobooks. This platform allows you to hire narrators who you can split royalties with or pay them a one time fee. The typical rate is $50 per finished hour of audio. Outside of Amazon, you can use platforms such as Findaway Voices to publish audiobooks. This gets your book into a wider variety of stores, such as Barnes and Noble, and includes Amazon distribution as well.

Just like the other two business models require you to conduct keyword and product research, book publishing also requires you to figure out which keywords are profitable. This is pretty easily done. Search for a keyword from Amazon's search box and filter for results in the Kindle store. Look at the BSRs of the first few results and see how many results in total come up. If the number of results is under 2,000 and if the BSRs are low enough, you can be assured that this is a profitable keyword to publish into. Amazon expects you to spend heavily on ads to push your book's sales on its platform.

Due to this, your overall profits might be reduced. It's best to rely on sending traffic of your own to your book listing. This is done by contacting book reviewers and influencers in your niche and sending them early edition copies of your book. Ask them to leave a review on Amazon as well as on their channels and tell them to direct people to buy your book. This will increase your profits massively. Amazon pays 40% royalties on paperback books and 70% royalties on ebooks. Audiobooks payment varies since ACX determines the price and pays you based on the subscription the user buys. It's possible to build a brand using KDP and to drum up some business for your content creation. If you already have content creation channels, then driving traffic to your book should be easy. While you cannot scale a KDP business as easily or profitably as an e-commerce business, you can make a lot of money nonetheless.

Conclusion

As you arrive at the end of this book, you'll now realize that creating passive income isn't as difficult a task as it first seemed. Sure, you'll need to work hard at it, but everything worth having requires hard work. The key to passive income success is your mindset. Approach things the right way, and you'll find it easy to create passive income. There are many vehicles you can use to generate passive income. The stock market and real estate are two of the most widely used options, but don't forget the humble savings account or a certificate of deposit. These might not pay you enough to beat inflation, but they still pay you something.

Investing in the stock market might seem intimidating, but you can create a completely passive income structure by choosing to invest in ETFs that follow an indexing strategy. There are active methods of making money in stocks that involve trading as well. While it is possible to be profitable doing this, the odds of success are low. However, if you succeed, you can make tons of money. Real estate offers many ways for you to make money. Some strategies might be too complex for you, but there are enough beginner-friendly strategies to get started with. If physical property isn't your thing, then investing in REITs, tax liens, deeds, or mortgage notes might prove to be a better fit.

Lastly, online business models are some of the most powerful ways to generate passive income. These require some work up front, but once you put the work in, you'll find that they'll generate tons of income for you to the point where you might even be in a position to quit your day job. Every single one of these methods requires you to conduct thorough research and to maintain a great mindset. You might fail at some of these, but you're sure to succeed at others. Maintain the right perspective throughout your journey, and you'll find that passive income comes to you without any trouble.

It's now time for you to take action on the advice provided in this book. I'm positive that the material in this book has the potential to change your life. Let me know what you think by leaving me a review on Amazon. As for now, I wish you the best of luck and encourage you to put your plans into action!

References

Clear, J. (2014, January 23). *The Marshmallow Experiment and the Power of Delayed Gratification*. James Clear. https://jamesclear.com/delayed-gratification

Earned Income | Internal Revenue Service. (2020, January 1). Www.Irs.Gov. https://www.irs.gov/credits-deductions/individuals/earned-income-tax-credit/earned-income

El-Sibaie, A. (2019, November 14). *2020 Tax Brackets*. Tax Foundation. https://taxfoundation.org/2020-tax-brackets/

FHA Loan Refinance and Home Purchase Loans at FHA.com. (2020, January 1). Www.Fha.Com. https://www.fha.com/fha_credit_requirements.

Financials & Accounting | Tesla, Inc. (2019). Tesla, Inc. https://ir.tesla.com/financial-information/quarterly-results

Kagan, J. (2020, February 3). *Individual Retirement Account (IRA)*. Investopedia. https://www.investopedia.com/terms/i/ira.asp

Martin, E. (2019, June 28). *Here's how many Americans have nothing saved for retirement*. CNBC. https://www.cnbc.com/2019/06/27/how-many-americans-have-nothing-saved-for-retirement.html

Mclean, B., & Elkind, P. (2004). *The smartest guys in the room : the amazing rise and scandalous fall of Enron*. Portfolio.

Passive Income. (2003, November 25). Investopedia. https://www.investopedia.com/terms/p/passiveincome.asp

Royal, J. (2020, February 4). *What Is A SEP IRA? A Complete Guide*. Bankrate. https://www.bankrate.com/retirement/sep-ira/

Schroeder, A. (2009). *The snowball : Warren Buffett and the business of life*. Bantam Books.

S&P 500 Historical Annual Returns. (2009). Macrotrends.Net. https://www.macrotrends.net/2526/sp-500-historical-annual-returns

Image Reference List

ask-sign-design-creative. (n.d.). https://pixabay.com/photos/ask-sign-design-creative-2341784/

bank-note-dollar-usd-us-dollar. (n.d.). https://pixabay.com/photos/bank-note-dollar-usd-us-dollar-941246/

chart-trading-courses-forex. (n.d.-a). https://pixabay.com/photos/chart-trading-courses-forex-1905225/

chart-trading-courses-forex. (n.d.-b). https://pixabay.com/photos/chart-trading-courses-forex-1905224/

coins-currency-investment-insurance. (n.d.). https://pixabay.com/photos/coins-currency-investment-insurance-948603/

house-home-porch-residence. (n.d.). https://pixabay.com/photos/house-home-porch-residence-186400/

house-real-estate-building. (n.d.). https://pixabay.com/photos/house-real-estate-building-1353389/

house-villa-villa-finale. (n.d.). https://pixabay.com/photos/house-villa-villa-finale-1620736/

money-finance-business-success. (n.d.). https://pixabay.com/photos/money-finance-business-success-2696234/

money-finance-wealth-currency. (n.d.). https://pixabay.com/photos/money-finance-wealth-currency-163502/

money-grow-interest-save-invest. (2020). https://pixabay.com/photos/money-grow-interest-save-invest-1604921/

money-profit-finance-business. (n.d.). https://pixabay.com/photos/money-profit-finance-business-2696219/

office-startup-business-home-office. (n.d.). https://pixabay.com/photos/office-startup-business-home-office-594132/

person-old-woman-grandma-senio. (n.d.). https://pixabay.com/photos/person-old-woman-grandma-senior-731423/

roll-the-dice-craps-board-game. (n.d.). https://pixabay.com/photos/roll-the-dice-craps-board-game-1502706/

snow-ice-freedom-shackles-clamps. (n.d.). https://pixabay.com/photos/snow-ice-freedom-shackles-clamps-3108069/

stock-exchange-trading-floor. (n.d.). https://pixabay.com/photos/stock-exchange-trading-floor-738671/

success-stairs-board-drawing. (n.d.). https://pixabay.com/photos/success-stairs-board-drawing-4168389/

twitter-facebook-together. (n.d.). https://pixabay.com/photos/twitter-facebook-together-292994/

wallet-credit-card-cash-investment. (n.d.). https://pixabay.com/photos/wallet-credit-card-cash-investment-2292428/

write-plan-desk-notes-pen-writing. (n.d.). https://pixabay.com/photos/write-plan-desk-notes-pen-writing-593333/

www.ingramcontent.com/pod-product-compliance
Lightning Source LLC
Chambersburg PA
CBHW060359080526
44583CB00012B/383